THE AUSTRALIAN
Women's Weekly

Easy
Microwave
Meals

Contents

tips & techniques 4

soups & stocks 12

main meals 24

side dishes 64

cooking vegetables 84

sweet treats 86

preserves 104

glossary 116

index 118

conversion charts 120

The days when a microwave sat in the corner waiting to reheat leftovers, are long gone. A microwave is an essential piece of kitchen equipment – for cooking in its own right. A key to success with your microwave is knowing what it will cook well and conversely, what it cooks less well. Look at the hints and tips on the next few pages in conjunction with your manufacturer's guide and see how much more you can get out of your microwave!

Pamela Clark

Food director

Tips & techniques

We take the mystery out of microwave cooking in this section with preparation and cooking techniques, hints on how to convert conventional recipes for use in the microwave oven, cookware options, tips and much more. Once you master the art of microwave cooking, you'll fall in love with this no-fuss, no-mess style of cooking.

A microwave oven is an essential appliance in every kitchen. You can cook practically anything in a modern microwave oven, thanks to the technological advances in their manufacture over the past few years. So, if you're one of the old school who believes that microwave ovens are only good for defrosting or reheating, think again!

Two common complaints about microwave cooking are the lack of browning of meat and the pale, unsavoury appearance of cakes. But there are some simple solutions to these problems.

Meat, even when fully cooked, has a dull, grey appearance. Experienced cooks know how to fix this problem easily with browning agents. No, these browning agents are not special products you'll have to buy. You will probably have a variety of browning products in your pantry, among them soy, teriyaki and barbecue sauces, jams, chutneys and brown sugar. Simply brush the surface of the meat with sauce or a marinade mixture before cooking.

Of course, using a recipe that suits microwave cooking is your best starting point.

POWER LEVELS
All our recipes have been triple-tested using a 900-watt microwave oven. Higher wattage ovens cook faster than lower wattage ovens so, since our recipes were made in a 900-watt oven, you'll have to check the instruction booklet of your own microwave oven and adjust cooking times accordingly.

Cooking bacon rashers (see page 11)

preparation & cooking techniques

A number of factors determine how long and how well things cook, among them the size and shape of food, the type of dish used and even how the food is arranged in the dish. Also, food placed in the microwave oven straight from the fridge will take longer to heat than food at room temperature.

MICROWAVE ENERGY

Food in your microwave oven is penetrated from all angles by microwaves, causing water and fat molecules in the food to vibrate rapidly. This friction creates the heat that cooks the food. This action continues for some time after the food is removed from the oven, which is why it continues to cook (see standing time, page 7). Because food cooks from the outer edges towards the centre, and as microwaves only penetrate to a depth of about 4cm, some recipes may overcook around the outside edges before the centre is done. That's why stirring, turning, shielding and arranging food is so important.

A microwave cake (above) can look magnificent (right).

FOOD DENSITY & COMPOSITION

● Solid, dense foods (such as meat and potatoes) take longer to cook than airy, porous foods (such as cakes, bread and minced meat).
● Fat and sugar attract microwaves, so foods with high levels of either cook and reheat more rapidly, and at a higher temperature, than water-based foods.
● Because bones conduct heat, meat on the bone will cook more quickly than boneless cuts. Also, the section of meat near the bone will cook faster than the rest, so you may need to shield the bony part of chops

PERFECTING CAKE-BAKING IN YOUR MICROWAVE
Baking cakes in the microwave oven has often led to disappointing results as they tend to be pale in colour and not very appealing. This is because the porous, airy texture of cakes means they cook in a very short time – and don't brown. But the benefits of microwave baking – including dramatically reduced baking times, easier recipes and power savings – outweigh the problems. Just choose a recipe that will produce a moist cake and then simply improve the appearance by dusting the cake with icing sugar, cocoa powder or cinnamon sugar. You can also use toasted, shredded or desiccated coconut (before or after cooking), finely chopped toasted nuts (before cooking), or spread the cake with cream cheese frosting, melted chocolate, or icing (after cooking).

and chicken drumsticks with small pieces of foil to prevent overcooking (see metal and aluminium foil, page 9).

• Sugary fillings in pies and pastries, cakes and jams become extremely hot much faster than the outside, so take care when testing and eating to avoid being burnt.

SIZE & SHAPE OF FOOD

• Smaller pieces of food cook faster than large ones, so it's best to cut your ingredients into similar-size pieces to ensure even cooking. A whole chicken, for example, will cook and begin to dry out around the breast area before the centre is cooked through. Chicken pieces, on the other hand, will cook more evenly.

• Food can naturally be an odd shape and may require special attention to ensure even cooking. A fish fillet, for example, may need to be shielded at the thinner end to prevent overcooking.

• Place the thickest part of fish/meat etc, to the outside of the turntable, where the energy source is greatest, and the thinner end to the middle, or tuck it under.

• Do not overload your microwave oven by cooking large amounts of food because the cooking time will increase and the food may not cook evenly.

• Cakes should always be cooked in a ring, loaf or shallow, round microwave-safe pan. Make your own ring dish by placing a glass, right-way up, in the centre of a 20cm round microwave-safe dish before you fill it with the cake mixture.

ARRANGING & STIRRING FOOD

Arranging food is just as important as choosing an appropriate dish.

• Arrange food in the microwave according to size and shape, with the thickest parts positioned towards the outside of the turntable and thin portions with bone closest to the centre.

• When reheating, make sure that thick, dense pieces of food are towards the outside of the plate or dish.

• Elevating thick cuts of meat on a roasting rack will help even cooking.

• Stir foods during cooking for even heating. Stir from the outside edge of the dish to transfer the food from the centre to the outside.

• Turn thick portions of meat, chicken, vegetables etc, once to ensure even cooking.

• Check cakes twice as they bake, as they can cook unevenly. Rotate the pan once during cooking to ensure even cooking.

• Food with a skin, membrane or other casing should be pierced in several places with a skewer to allow the steam to escape. If the skin is not pierced, the food may burst. Always pierce egg yolks when poaching eggs and when cooking sausages, chicken or vegetables with the skin left on.

COOKING VEGETABLES

Perfect microwave vegies are easy. Just chop vegetables into evenly sized pieces and place those that take longer to cook around the outer edge of the dish. Vegetables requiring less cooking time are placed inside. Don't forget to include standing time when you calculate how long your vegetables need to cook.

It's important to remember that food continues to cook after it is removed from the microwave because the molecules are still vibrating. That's why many recipes include standing times in addition to cooking times. Standing times vary, usually 5 to 10 minutes depending on the food. Always test your food at the end of the cooking and standing time, then, if extra cooking is necessary, it should be done in short bursts (seconds rather than minutes) to avoid overcooking.

● Cakes will continue to cook for a long period due to their high sugar content and airy texture – allow about 10 minutes.

● Meat should be slightly undercooked to your preference, then covered and left to stand for 10 to 15 minutes to finish cooking.

● Green vegetables cook quickly and can easily be overcooked. They should always be cooked covered, unless the recipe states otherwise, and undercooked if they are to be reheated before serving. They will remain hot for around 5 minutes if kept covered after being removed from the microwave.

DEFROSTING

Defrosting in the microwave is a quick and hygienic way to thaw food. Bacteria does not find the temperature warm and stable enough to grow. The defrost function button is automatically programmed to a medium

The use of aluminium foil – around the bone ends of chicken drumsticks and in the corners of a meatloaf – will prevent the food from burning, drying out and overcooking.

temperature suitable for defrosting.

● Foods with high fat content or less density towards the edges, such as minced steak or chicken pieces, attract microwaves and may start to cook around the outside. To prevent this, place evenly sized, trimmed portions of meat (unwrapped) around the edge of the turntable and remove any defrosted portions of mince during the defrosting programme.

● Remember to also consider the standing time when defrosting meat. Remove the meat before it thaws out completely and allow about another 15 minutes standing time.

● If larger pieces of meat start to cook around the edges, try using an even lower temperature than defrost, such as LOW (10%), and turn the meat over once during defrosting.

REHEATING

Reheating a meal in the microwave oven isn't only convenient – it also saves on washing up, as meals can be ready in minutes on the serving plate. Food placed in the microwave straight from the fridge will take longer to reheat than food at room temperature. Try using a lower heat setting; it may take a little longer, but the results will reflect the more even heat distribution.

what cookware to use?

You can buy cookware designed specifically for microwaves but you will probably have suitable dishes already. For example, Pyrex, glass and some ceramic and plastic dishes are suitable.

• Always test any cookware not labelled 'microwave-safe' by filling a microwave-safe jug with 1 cup of cold water and placing it in the microwave with the dish to be tested. Heat on HIGH (100%) 1 minute. If the dish remains cold (while the water is warm), it's safe to use. If the water is still cool and the dish hot, the dish is not suitable.

• Unsuitable dishes may overheat and break, warp or cause burns if you remove them without an oven-mitt.

• Some cookware – including styrofoam and polystyrene containers, bone china, ice-cream and plastic takeaway containers – should only be used for very short periods (2 minutes max.).

• It's best to use round or oval dishes in the microwave as the food cooks more evenly.

• Rectangular dishes often need small pieces of foil in the corners to prevent overcooking.

ovenproof glass Ordinary glassware, bottles and jars can be used to reheat food for short periods (5 minutes max.). The most useful glass for microwave use is Pyrex.

china, porcelain & ceramics Most suitable ovenware dishes will be labelled microwave-safe.

• Delicate china and dinnerware marked ovenproof is usually safe to use, but never use china with a metallic trim, or containers with metal parts.

• Do not use any repaired china as the glue will melt.

stoneware & pottery Pottery which has been glazed completely inside and out, with no metallic glaze or trim, is suitable for microwave use.

• Don't use pottery or stoneware which is not completely covered with glaze unless it is marked microwave-safe, as it may absorb moisture, become extremely hot, cause crazing and eventually crack. If unsure, test it before use.

plastic Plastic microwave-safe cookware is ideal for baking and shorter cooking periods.

• However, some plastic containers may burn or scorch if used for foods with high fat content, such as cheese, or high sugar content, such as jam and sweet fillings.

• Melamine dinnerware can be used at low temperatures and for short cooking times (2 minutes max.) but may melt or break if overheated.

• Ice-cream, plastic takeaway, polystyrene or styrofoam containers can become soft or melt with long cooking times. They should only be used to reheat food for very short periods (2 minutes max.).

cling film There is a special film designed specifically for microwave use. While a little more expensive than conventional film, it's worth the investment.

• When removing cling film from a microwaved dish, carefully peel it from the back of the dish to protect your hands and face from steam.

Oven bags and some freezer bags can be used; check the manufacturer's instructions.

Do not use wire twists in the microwave; cut a narrow strip off the edge of an oven bag and use it as a tie.

wood & paper Wooden bowls or boards shouldn't be used in the microwave oven as they may dry out and crack.

Wicker or straw baskets can be used to warm bread rolls for very short periods; long cooking times will cause varnish on baskets to crack.

Use wooden skewers when cooking kebabs in the microwave oven.

Absorbent papers (like paper towels) can be used for short cooking times to avoid splatters.

Baking parchment can be used to prevent food sticking.

To be safe, always check the manufacturer's instructions for microwave suitability; some recycled brands of paperware may contain metal fragments.

metal & aluminium foil Metal cookware, dishes or utensils should never be used in the microwave under any circumstances. Aluminium foil is the only metal-based product that can be used, but only in very small amounts.

Never cover completely food with foil; it's only safe to cover up to one-third of food and you should never let it touch the walls of the oven.

As microwaves cannot penetrate foil, small, smooth pieces of foil can be used as a shield to prevent food over-cooking around the edges.

Foil trays and containers can be used only when the volume of food is at least double the amount of foil (eg. 70% food to 30% foil). The container should be no more than 2cm high and sit at least 3cm from the oven walls. Do not use the foil lids that come with foil trays and fold down any sharp edges at the top of the foil container.

If a metal utensil or too much foil is used, or if a foil container comes in contact with the walls, then arcing (sparks) will occur. If this happens, stop the oven immediately, remove the metal or reduce the quantity of foil used. Continued arcing will damage your microwave.

CONVERTING RECIPES

You can't convert all recipes to make them suitable for microwave cooking, but there are many where it's a simple matter of reducing the liquid or cooking time.

Reduce the amounts of additional liquid.

As a guide, reduce fats or oils in recipes to a maximum of 40g or 2 tablespoons.

Reduce the addition of flavourings and seasonings.

Reduce cooking times by about one-third – not forgetting standing time. Extra time can be added in very short bursts if necessary.

Cut food into evenly sized pieces and cook in batches.

Dishes topped with cheese or breadcrumbs should be browned under a grill before serving.

Large cuts of meat are best browned on the hob before cooking in the microwave.

Dos and Don'ts

DON'T overcook food. The best advice is to undercook all food, check whether the food is done and, if extra cooking is required, do so in very short bursts only.

DON'T shallow- or deep-fry in the microwave as the oil can boil and splatter, causing burns.

DO a quick test of all cookware to determine if suitable for use in the microwave oven.

DON'T boil eggs in their shell as they will explode.

DO take care when cooking a whole chicken. After cooking, check the internal temperature has reached 87°C.

DON'T use conventional meat thermometers inside a microwave. Use them only to test meat after it is out of the oven. You can buy microwave thermometers that remain in food during cooking.

DO make sure when shielding food with small amounts of foil that only a maximum of one-third of food is ever covered with the foil.

DON'T ever allow foil or foil trays to touch oven walls, and never cover food entirely with foil.

DO check the wattage of your own microwave oven. Our recipes have been triple-tested in a 900-watt microwave. High-wattage ovens cook faster than low-wattage ovens so adjust cooking times accordingly.

how do I...

melt gelatine? Sprinkle 2 teaspoons of gelatine over 1 tablespoon water in small microwave-safe bowl; cook, uncovered, on MEDIUM (55%) about 30 seconds or until dissolved.

clarify butter? Place 125g butter in microwave-safe bowl; cook, uncovered, on MEDIUM-LOW (30%) about 3 minutes or until foaming. Skim foam from surface of butter. Stand butter for 2 minutes before spooning clear liquid into a glass bowl.

soften lumpy sugar? To soften 1 cup (200g) lumpy, hard brown sugar, place in a microwave-safe bowl with a thick slice of apple on top; cook, covered, on HIGH (100%) about 30 seconds. Stand, covered, 5 minutes before using sugar.

warm plates? To warm dinner plates for serving, place a damp piece of absorbent paper between each plate in stack of four. Place the four stacked plates on turntable; heat for 1 minute on HIGH (100%). Do not use plates with a metallic trim.

toast coconut? To toast 45g coconut, place in a microwave-safe glass dish; cook, uncovered, on HIGH (100%) about 5 minutes or until browned lightly, stirring twice during cooking.

toast almonds? To toast 100g slivered, flaked or whole almonds, place in a large, shallow microwave-safe glass dish; cook, uncovered, on HIGH (100%) about 3 minutes or until browned lightly, stirring twice during cooking.

rehydrate sun-dried tomatoes? Place 1 cup sun-dried tomatoes in a small microwave-safe glass bowl with 2 tablespoons of red wine or water. Cook, covered, on MEDIUM-HIGH (70%) for 3 minutes, stirring once.

pop corn? Place 130g of popping corn in an oven bag or paper bag; secure bag loosely with kitchen string. Place bag on turntable; cook, on MEDIUM-HIGH (70%) for about 4 minutes or until popped. Remove bag from microwave with tongs; stand for 2 minutes before opening.

soften crystallised honey? Place jar (without lid) in microwave oven; cook, uncovered, on HIGH (100%) about 30 seconds or until honey liquidises.

cook prawn crackers? Place 10 prawn crackers around the edge of turntable; cook, uncovered, on HIGH (100%) about 30 seconds or until puffed.

scramble eggs? Melt a teaspoon of butter in a microwave-safe bowl; add 2 eggs, whisk until frothy. Cook, uncovered, on HIGH (100%) for 1½ minutes or until just firm, stirring twice during cooking. Stand for 1 minute.

poach an egg? Place 2 teaspoons water in a microwave-safe bowl; cook, uncovered, on HIGH (100%) for 30 seconds. Add egg to bowl, prick egg yolk; cook, covered, on MEDIUM (55%) for 40 seconds or until set. Stand for 30 seconds; drain and invert onto serving plate.

cook poppadums? Place 2 poppadums at a time on turntable; cook, uncovered, on HIGH (100%) about 30 seconds or until puffed.

dry breadcrumbs? To dry 70g stale bread-crumbs, place on a microwave-safe glass plate; cook, uncovered, on HIGH (100%) about 2 minutes or until dry, stirring once during cooking.

make porridge for one? To make 1 serve of porridge, place ⅓ cup rolled oats in microwave-safe bowl with 250ml water. Cook, uncovered, on HIGH (100%) for 2 minutes, stirring once during cooking.

cook beans and pulses? Rinse and place 1 cup soaked beans or pulses in a large microwave-safe bowl with 4 cups boiling water. Cook, uncovered, on HIGH (100%) for 45 minutes or until tender.

toast sesame seeds? To toast 35g sesame seeds, place in a microwave-safe bowl; cook, uncovered, on HIGH (100%) about 4 minutes or until browned lightly, stirring twice during cooking.

melt marshmallows? To melt 100g marshmallows, place in a small microwave-safe bowl; cook, uncovered, on HIGH (100%) for about 30 seconds to serve with hot chocolate.

soften ice-cream? Loosen lid of ice-cream container, place container on turntable; cook, on LOW (10%) about 2 minutes or until soft.

make a white sauce? Melt 60g butter in a microwave-safe bowl, add ¼ cup plain flour, mix to a smooth paste. Cook, uncovered, on HIGH (100%) for 1 minute. Gradually whisk in 2 cups milk. Cook, uncovered, on HIGH (100%) for 5 minutes, until sauce boils and thickens, whisking 3 times during cooking.

make custard? Blend ¼ cup custard powder, 2 table-spoons sugar with ½ cup milk to form a smooth paste in a microwave-safe bowl. Whisk in 1½ cups of milk; cook, uncovered, on HIGH (100%) for 6 minutes until thick and smooth, stirring 3 times.

cook potatoes? To cook a medium (250g) jacket potato, pierce skin with a fork to allow steam to escape. Cook, uncovered, on turntable on HIGH (100%), about 4 minutes or until potato softens.

caramelise onion? Combine 20g butter and 1 tablespoon brown sugar in a microwave-safe dish; cook, uncovered, on MEDIUM (55%) 30 seconds. Add 1 large onion, sliced thinly; stir until onion is coated with butter and sugar. Cook, uncovered, on HIGH (100%) for 8 minutes, stirring every 2 minutes during cooking.

soften dried fruit? To soften 190g dried fruit, place in a microwave-safe bowl with 60ml water; cook, covered, on HIGH (100%) about 3 minutes or until fruit is soft.

soften butter or cream cheese? Place (unwrapped) in a microwave-safe bowl; cook, uncovered, on MEDIUM-LOW (30%) about 10 seconds or until just softened.

steam handtowels? Roll 4 moistened cloth hand-towels and then place on microwave-safe plate; microwave, uncovered, on HIGH (100%) for 1 minute.

soften citrus fruit for juicing? To make citrus fruit squeeze easily, place fruit on turn-table; cook; uncovered, on HIGH (100%) for 20 seconds.

refresh stale bread rolls or potato crisps? Place 6 bread rolls around the outside of turntable; cook, uncovered, on HIGH (100%) about 30 seconds or until soft. Place 2 cups stale potato crisps in a thin layer on 2 sheets of absorbent paper on a microwave-safe plate; cook, uncovered, on HIGH (100%) about 30 seconds. Stand for 5 minutes.

cook bacon rashers? Place rashers bacon on a double layer of absorbent paper on microwave oven turntable. Cover with 2 more layers of absorbent paper. Cook on HIGH (100%) for 3 minutes or until cooked as desired.

improve the look of meat cooked in a microwave? Glaze meat with sauces such as teriyaki, Worcestershire, soy, hoisin and barbecue, or try chutney, marmalade and curry pastes. Dry spices such as paprika, seasoned coatings or stock powders may be sprinkled on chicken pieces, hamburgers and other cut meats.

Soups & stocks

combination short soup

1 medium (120g) carrot
2 litres chicken stock
250g spinach, shredded
200g Chinese barbecued
   pork, sliced
230g can sliced bamboo
   shoots, rinsed, drained
½ cup (40g) bean sprouts
4 spring onions, chopped
1 tablespoon soy sauce
wontons
150g minced pork
1 spring onion, chopped
1 clove garlic, crushed
1 tablespoon oyster sauce
16 gow gee wrappers
1 egg white, beaten lightly

1 Cut carrot into 4cm-long thin strips. Bring stock to boil in large microwave-safe bowl, covered, on HIGH (100%) about 10 minutes. Add wontons; cook, uncovered, on MEDIUM-HIGH (70%) about 4 minutes or until cooked through.
2 Add carrot and remaining ingredients; cook, uncovered, on MEDIUM-HIGH (70%) 2 minutes.

wontons combine mince, onion, garlic and sauce in small bowl. Brush each gow gee wrapper with egg white, place rounded teaspoons of mince mixture in centre of each round, pinch together to form pouches which enclose filling.

- **prep time: 55 minutes**
- **cook time: 20 minutes**
- **serves: 6**
- **per serve: 9.2g fat; 283 cal**
- **tip: ready-to-eat barbecued pork can be purchased from specialty Asian food stores and some supermarkets.**

Cook's tip

Here's a quick way to soak pulses to ready for cooking. Place 1 cup beans or pulses in a microwave-safe bowl, add 2 cups water; cook, covered, on HIGH (100%) for 5 minutes. Stir then cook, covered, on MEDIUM-LOW (30%) a further 30 minutes, stirring occasionally. The beans are now ready to cook in your favourite recipe.

sweet potato soup

1 teaspoon butter

2 teaspoons vegetable oil

1 medium (150g) brown onion, chopped

1 teaspoon grated fresh ginger

2 cloves garlic, crushed

½ teaspoon ground cumin

½ teaspoon ground coriander

1 large (500g) sweet potato, chopped

625ml chicken stock

1 teaspoon grated orange rind

2 teaspoons tomato paste

2 tablespoons soured cream

1 Combine butter, oil, onion, ginger, garlic and spices in large microwave-safe bowl; cook, uncovered, on HIGH (100%) 4 minutes, stirring once during cooking.

2 Add sweet potato and ½ cup (125ml) of the stock; cook, covered, on HIGH (100%) about 8 minutes or until sweet potato is tender, stirring once during cooking.

3 Blend or process sweet potato mixture, remaining stock, rind, paste and cream, in batches, until smooth.

4 Return soup to bowl; cook, covered, on MEDIUM-HIGH (70%) about 3 minutes or until hot, stirring once during cooking. Do not allow soup to boil.

- prep time: 25 minutes
- cook time: 20 minutes
- serves: 4
- per serve: 8.0g fat; 183 cal

coconut lentil soup

1   Combine butter, onion, ginger, garlic, chilli and spices in large microwave-safe bowl; cook, uncovered, on HIGH (100%) about 2 minutes or until onion is soft, stirring once during cooking.

2   Add lentils and stock; cook, covered, on HIGH (100%) about 10 minutes or until lentils are tender, stirring twice during cooking.

3   Stir in cream and extra water; blend or process soup mixture, in batches, until smooth.

4   Return soup to bowl with coriander; cook, uncovered, on MEDIUM (55%) about 3 minutes or until hot.

30g butter
1 medium (150g) brown
  onion, chopped finely
1 teaspoon grated fresh
  ginger
1 clove garlic, crushed
1 birdseye chilli, deseeded,
  chopped finely
½ teaspoon ground
  cardamom
½ teaspoon ground turmeric
1 cup (200g) red lentils
750ml chicken stock
½ cup (125ml) coconut
  cream
250ml water, extra
1 tablespoon chopped
  fresh coriander leaves

- prep time: 25 minutes
- cook time: 15 minutes
- serves: 4
- per serve: 13.9g fat;
  299 cal

chicken & corn soup

1.5 litres chicken stock
440g can creamed corn
1 teaspoon sesame oil
⅓ cup (50g) cornflour
⅓ cup (80ml) water
6 spring onions, sliced thinly
½ teaspoon grated fresh
  ginger
2 egg whites, beaten lightly
2 tablespoons water, extra
2 slices (45g) ham, sliced
  thinly
1 cup (170g) shredded
  cooked chicken
2 teaspoons soy sauce
3 spring onions, sliced thinly,
  extra

1 Heat stock, corn and oil in large microwave-safe bowl, covered, on HIGH (100%) 5 minutes, stirring once during cooking.
2 Stir in blended cornflour and water, then onion and ginger; cook, uncovered, on HIGH (100%) about 5 minutes or until soup boils and thickens slightly, stirring once during cooking.
3 Whisk combined egg white and extra water into hot soup in a thin stream. Stir in ham, chicken and soy; sprinkle with extra onion.

- **prep time: 30 minutes**
- **cook time: 10 minutes**
- **serves: 6**
- **per serve: 4.6g fat; 221 cal**

indian chowder

1 Combine butter, onion, garlic and bacon in large microwave-safe bowl; cook, uncovered, on HIGH (100%) 5 minutes, stirring once during cooking.

2 Reserve ¼ cup of the stock, add remaining stock to bowl with celery and sweet potato; cook, covered, on HIGH (100%) about 12 minutes or until vegetables are tender, stirring once during cooking.

3 Add blended flour and reserved stock to bowl with milk; cook, uncovered, on HIGH (100%) about 5 minutes or until chowder boils and thickens slightly, stirring once during cooking.

4 Place spinach in large microwave-safe bowl; cook, covered, on HIGH (100%) about 3 minutes or until wilted. Add spinach to chowder; sprinkle with nutmeg.

20g butter
1 medium (150g) brown onion, chopped
2 cloves garlic, crushed
3 bacon rashers, chopped
1½ cups (375ml) vegetable stock
2 trimmed (150g) celery sticks, chopped coarsely
1 large (500g) sweet potato, chopped coarsely
2 tablespoons plain flour
400ml coconut milk
500g spinach, trimmed
nutmeg

- prep time: 30 minutes
- cook time: 25 minutes
- serves: 4
- per serve: 133.8g fat; 455 cal

pumpkin soup with tortellini

250g beef tortellini
500ml boiling water
2 tablespoons olive oil
1 medium (150g) brown
    onion, chopped finely
1 clove garlic, crushed
½ teaspoon ground
    coriander
1 teaspoon ground cumin
1kg pumpkin, chopped
1 medium (200g) potato,
    chopped
1 litre chicken stock
½ cup (125ml) double cream
1 tablespoon chopped fresh
    chives
1 tablespoon chopped fresh
    basil leaves

1 Combine pasta with boiling water in medium microwave-safe bowl; cook, uncovered, on HIGH (100%) about 3 minutes or until tender, stirring once during cooking. Drain.

2 Combine oil, onion, garlic, coriander and cumin in large microwave-safe bowl; cook, uncovered, on HIGH (100%) 2 minutes, stirring once during cooking.

3 Stir in pumpkin, potato and stock; cook, covered, on HIGH (100%) about 10 minutes or until pumpkin is tender, stirring once during cooking. Stand 5 minutes.

4 Blend or process mixture, in batches, until smooth. Return soup to bowl with cream, herbs and pasta; cook, uncovered, on HIGH (100%) about 2 minutes or until heated through.

- **prep time: 30 minutes**
- **cook time: 25 minutes**
- **serves: 6**
- **per serve: 17.5g fat; 384 cal**
- **tip: you can use butternut squash instead of pumpkin, if you prefer.**

vegetable soup with pesto

30g butter
1 medium (120g) carrot,
    chopped coarsely
1 medium (200g) potato,
    chopped coarsely
60g green beans, chopped
    coarsely
1 medium (120g) courgette,
    chopped coarsely
1 medium (150g) brown
    onion, chopped finely
400g can tomatoes
2 tablespoons plain flour
2 tablespoons tomato paste
750ml vegetable stock
2 teaspoons sugar
300g can butter beans,
    rinsed, drained

pesto
1 cup firmly packed fresh
    basil leaves
250g spinach, trimmed
½ cup (40g) grated
    parmesan cheese
½ cup (80g) pine nuts
5 cloves garlic, quartered
½ cup (125ml) olive oil

1 Combine butter, fresh vegetables and undrained crushed tomatoes in large microwave-safe bowl; cook, covered, on HIGH (100%) 10 minutes.

2 Whisk in flour, paste, stock and sugar; cook, covered, on HIGH (100%) about 5 minutes or until vegetables are soft and soup boils and thickens, stirring twice during cooking.

3 Stir in butter beans. Serve soup topped with pesto.

pesto Blend or process basil, spinach, cheese, nuts and garlic until smooth, adding oil gradually in a thin stream while motor is operating.

- **prep time: 40 minutes**
- **cook time: 15 minutes**
- **serves: 4**
- **per serve: 55.2g fat; 653 cal**

mulligatawny soup

2 tablespoons madras curry
  paste
1 small (200g) leek, sliced
1 trimmed (75g) celery stick,
  chopped finely
1 medium (120g) carrot,
  chopped finely
2 cloves garlic, crushed
2 teaspoons grated fresh
  ginger
½ cup (100g) red lentils
1 litre vegetable stock
1½ cups (375ml) coconut
  milk
1 medium (150g) apple,
  peeled, grated
250g cooked roast beef,
  sliced
2 tablespoons lime juice
2 tablespoons chopped fresh
  coriander leaves

1 Combine paste, leek, celery, carrot, garlic and ginger in large microwave-safe bowl; cook, covered, on HIGH (100%) 4 minutes, stirring once during cooking.
2 Add lentils and stock; cook, covered, on HIGH (100%) 15 minutes, stirring once during cooking. Blend or process mixture, in batches, until smooth; return to bowl.
3 Add milk, apple and beef; cook soup, covered, on MEDIUM-HIGH (70%) 5 minutes. Stir in juice and coriander.

- **prep time: 30 minutes**
- **cook time: 25 minutes**
- **serves: 6**
- **per serve: 22.5g fat; 339 cal**

chicken minestrone

1   Combine chicken, onion, garlic, bacon, celery and carrot in large microwave-safe bowl; cook, covered, on MEDIUM-HIGH (70%) 15 minutes, stirring once during cooking.
2   Add undrained crushed tomatoes, beans, stock and pasta; cook, uncovered, on MEDIUM-HIGH (70%) about 10 minutes or until pasta is just tender. Stir in herbs.

500g chicken thigh
   fillets, chopped
1 medium (150g) brown
   onion, sliced
1 clove garlic, crushed
2 bacon rashers, chopped
1 trimmed (75g) celery
   stick, chopped
1 medium (120g) carrot,
   chopped coarsely
400g can tomatoes
300g can kidney beans,
   rinsed, drained
3 cups (750ml) chicken
   stock
40g macaroni
2 tablespoons chopped
   fresh oregano
1 tablespoon chopped
   fresh flat-leaf parsley

prep time: 25 minutes
cook time: 25 minutes
serves: 4
per serve: 10.3g fat;
364 cal

stocks

- **These recipes can be made up to 4 days ahead and stored, covered, in the refrigerator.**
- **Be sure to remove any fat from the surface after the cooled stock has been refrigerated overnight. If the stock is to be kept longer, it is best to freeze it in smaller quantities. Freezing stock in an ice-cube tray results in convenient and easy-to-use portions.**
- **Ready-made stock is available in cartons or sachets in most supermarkets. Stock cubes or powder can also be used. As a guide, 1 teaspoon of stock powder or 1 small crumbled stock cube mixed with 1 cup (250ml) water will give a fairly strong stock.**
- **Be aware of the salt and fat content of stock cubes and powders and prepared stocks.**

beef stock

375g beef bones
1 litre water
1 bayleaf
1 onion, peeled and chopped

1 Combine beef bones, the water, bayleaf and onion in large bowl; cover.
2 Cook on HIGH until stock boils; cook for further 5 minutes on HIGH.
3 Remove bones, allow to cool. Cover, and refrigerate; skim off any fat when cold. Can be frozen once cold.

chicken stock

1kg chicken bones or carcass
1 litre water
1 onion, peeled and chopped
1 stick of celery

1 Place chicken bones in a 2.5 litre dish with the water. Add onion and celery.
2 Cover tightly and cook on HIGH for 30 minutes.
3 Remove bones, allow to cool. Cover, and refrigerate; skim off any fat when cold. Can be frozen once cold.

main meals

chicken with lemon mustard sauce

30g butter

1 tablespoon vegetable oil

1 medium (150g) brown
onion, sliced

1 clove garlic, crushed

4 (680g) chicken breast fillets

2 teaspoons sweet paprika

300ml double cream

1 teaspoon finely grated
lemon rind

2 teaspoons lemon juice

2 teaspoons wholegrain
mustard

1 chicken stock cube

2 teaspoons cornflour

1 tablespoon water

2 tablespoons finely
chopped fresh chives

1 Combine butter, oil, onion and garlic in large shallow microwave-safe dish; cook, uncovered, on HIGH (100%) 4 minutes, stirring once during cooking. Remove onion mixture from dish.

2 Place chicken in same dish; sprinkle with paprika. Cook, covered, on MEDIUM-HIGH (70%) about 10 minutes or until cooked through. Remove chicken from dish; cover to keep warm.

3 Return onion mixture to same dish with cream, rind, juice, mustard, crumbled stock cube and blended cornflour and the water; cook, uncovered, on HIGH (100%) about 3 minutes or until sauce boils and thickens slightly, stirring once during cooking. Stir chives through sauce; serve with chicken.

- prep time: 25 minutes
- cook time: 20 minutes
- serves: 4
- per serve: 47.5g fat;
  612 cal

Cook's tip

Here's a quick and easy way to crisp bacon for use in a recipe. Chop 3 rashers of bacon finely, place on a microwave-safe plate between double thicknesses of absorbent paper then cook on HIGH (100%) for 3 minutes. Just right to sprinkle on top of baked potatoes or a casserole.

coq au vin

20g butter

8 (880g) chicken thigh fillets, halved

2 cloves garlic, crushed

3 bacon rashers, chopped

10 (250g) spring onions, trimmed

200g chestnut brown mushrooms, halved

2 tablespoons brandy

½ cup (125ml) dry red wine

½ cup (125ml) chicken stock

1 sprig fresh flat-leaf parsley

2 teaspoons chopped fresh thyme

1 bay leaf

2 tablespoons tomato paste

2 tablespoons cornflour

2 tablespoons water

1 Combine butter, chicken, garlic, bacon and onions in 3-litre shallow microwave-safe dish; cook, covered, on MEDIUM-HIGH (70%) 15 minutes, stirring once during cooking.

2 Stir in mushrooms, brandy, wine, stock, herbs, bay leaf and paste; cook, covered, on MEDIUM-HIGH (70%) about 10 minutes or until chicken is very tender, stirring once during cooking.

3 Stir blended cornflour blended and the water into mixture in dish; cook, uncovered, on MEDIUM-HIGH (70%) about 2 minutes or until mixture boils and thickens slightly.

- prep time: 25 minutes
- cook time: 30 minutes
- serves: 6
- per serve: 12.7g fat; 312 cal

chicken & apricot tagine

1 Combine oil, chicken, garlic, onion and spices in large microwave-safe bowl; cook, covered, on MEDIUM-HIGH (70%) 15 minutes, stirring once during cooking.

2 Add stock, honey and apricots; cook, uncovered, on MEDIUM-HIGH (70%) about 5 minutes or until apricots are tender. Stir in blended cornflour and the water; cook, uncovered, on MEDIUM-HIGH (70%) about 3 minutes or until mixture boils and thickens slightly, whisking once during cooking.

3 Cook nuts on microwave-safe plate, uncovered, on HIGH (100%) about 3 minutes or until browned lightly, stirring twice during cooking. Stir nuts and coriander into tagine.

1 tablespoon olive oil
1kg chicken thigh fillets, chopped
2 cloves garlic, crushed
1 large (200g) brown onion, chopped finely
¼ teaspoon ground cinnamon
½ teaspoon ground cumin
½ teaspoon ground ginger
½ teaspoon ground turmeric
1 cup (250ml) hot chicken stock
1 tablespoon honey
1 cup (150g) dried apricots
1 tablespoon cornflour
1 tablespoon water
½ cup (80g) blanched almonds
2 tablespoons chopped fresh coriander leaves

- prep time: 25 minutes
- cook time: 30 minutes
- serves: 4
- per serve: 26.8g fat; 585 cal

florentine chicken mozzarella

250g frozen spinach, thawed
4 (680g) chicken breast fillets
1 tablespoon olive oil
120g mozzarella cheese,
    sliced thinly
600ml bottled chunky tomato
    pasta sauce
1 tablespoon chopped fresh
    basil leaves

1 Drain spinach then, using hand, squeeze out excess liquid; chop spinach coarsely.

2 Brush chicken with oil and place in large shallow microwave-safe dish; cook, covered, on MEDIUM-HIGH (70%) about 8 minutes or until almost cooked through. Drain away the liquid.

3 Top chicken with spinach then cheese. Pour combined sauce and basil into dish; cook, uncovered, on MEDIUM (55%) about 8 minutes or until cheese melts and sauce is hot.

- prep time: 15 minutes
- cook time: 20 minutes
- serves: 4
- per serve: 16.7g fat;
  420 cal

tasty coated chicken

1 Discard chicken skin. Toss chicken in combined flour, powders and salts; shake away excess. Dip chicken into combined egg and milk, then coat in crumbs. Cover; refrigerate 1 hour.

2 Melt butter in small microwave-safe bowl, uncovered, on HIGH (100%) 1 minute.

3 Cover microwave oven turntable with 2 layers of absorbent paper; place chicken in single layer on paper. Brush chicken lightly with butter, cover with 2 layers of absorbent paper. Cook on MEDIUM-HIGH (70%) 8 minutes.

4 Rotate chicken pieces, re-cover with paper; cook on MEDIUM-HIGH (70%) about 8 minutes or until cooked through.

8 (1.3kg) chicken thigh cutlets
2 tablespoons plain flour
2 tablespoons chicken stock powder
½ teaspoon five-spice powder
1 teaspoon garlic salt
1 teaspoon celery salt
1 egg
2 tablespoons milk
¾ cup (75g) corn flakes, crushed into crumbs
60g butter

- prep time: 25 minutes (plus chilling time)
- cook time: 20 minutes
- serves: 4
- per serve: 26.1g fat; 760 cal

thai-style chicken curry

1 tablespoon vegetable oil

1 tablespoon Thai red curry
   paste

500g chicken thigh fillets,
   sliced thickly

160ml coconut milk

1 tablespoon fish sauce

4 spring onions, sliced thinly

230g can sliced bamboo
   shoots, rinsed, drained

1 tablespoon coarsely
   chopped fresh basil leaves

1 Combine oil and paste in large microwave-safe bowl;
cook, covered, on HIGH (100%) about 1 minute or until
fragrant.

2 Add chicken; cook, covered, on MEDIUM-HIGH (70%)
about 8 minutes or until cooked through, gently stirring
once during cooking.

3 Add milk, sauce, onion and bamboo shoots; cook,
uncovered, on MEDIUM (55%) about 4 minutes or until
heated through. Stir in basil.

- prep time: 20 minutes
- cook time: 15 minutes
- serves: 4
- per serve: 20.8g fat;
  318 cal

asian-style chilli drumsticks

1 Combine chicken in large bowl with sauces, honey, garlic, ginger and spice in large bowl, cover; refrigerate several hours.

2 Drain chicken over microwave-safe bowl; reserve marinade.

3 Place chicken, in single layer, in large shallow microwave-safe dish, with thick ends toward edge of dish; brush with 1 tablespoon marinade. Cook, uncovered, on MEDIUM-HIGH (70%) about 20 minutes or until chicken is cooked through.

4 Place sesame seeds on microwave-safe plate; cook, uncovered, on HIGH (100%) about 3 minutes or until browned lightly, stirring twice during cooking.

5 Cook remaining marinade, uncovered, on HIGH (100%) about 2 minutes or until marinade boils and thickens slightly; brush over cooked chicken. Sprinkle with seeds.

8 (1.2kg) chicken drumsticks
2 tablespoons sweet chilli sauce
¼ cup (60ml) hoisin sauce
2 tablespoons honey
3 cloves garlic, crushed
1 teaspoon grated fresh ginger
¼ teaspoon five-spice powder
1 tablespoon sesame seeds

prep time: 10 minutes
(plus marinating time)
cook time: 25 minutes
serves: 4
per serve: 20.3 fat; 401 cal

chicken, bean & sausage casserole

3 bacon rashers, sliced

2 thin (165g) spicy Italian sausages

2 thin (100g) beef sausages

9 (1kg) chicken thigh fillets, halved

2 cloves garlic, crushed

3 cloves

12 black peppercorns

1 trimmed (75g) stick celery, sliced

4 medium (480g) carrots, sliced

2 medium (300g) onions, sliced

300g can butter beans, rinsed, drained

½ cup (125ml) dry white wine

½ cup (125ml) chicken stock

2 tablespoons tomato paste

1 Cook bacon between double thicknesses of absorbent paper (see page 11), on HIGH (100%) about 5 minutes or until crisp. Drain on absorbent paper; reserve.

2 Prick sausages with fork, place in 3-litre shallow microwave-safe dish, cover with sheet of absorbent paper; cook on MEDIUM-HIGH (70%) about 5 minutes or until cooked through. Cool sausages; slice thickly.

3 Add chicken to same dish; cook, covered, on MEDIUM-HIGH (70%) 10 minutes, stirring once during cooking.

4 Add garlic, cloves, peppercorns, celery, carrot, onion, beans, wine, stock and paste; cook, covered, on MEDIUM-HIGH (70%) about 20 minutes or until chicken and vegetables are very tender, stirring once during cooking. Stir in sausage; serve casserole sprinkled with bacon.

- prep time: 30 minutes
- cook time: 40 minutes
- serves: 6
- per serve: 20.6g fat; 419 cal

honey mustard chicken with fruity couscous

1 Combine honey, mustard, juice and rosemary in large shallow microwave-safe dish; cook, uncovered, on HIGH (100%) 2 minutes.

2 Add chicken, in single layer, to dish, cook, uncovered, on MEDIUM-HIGH (70%) about 10 minutes or until chicken is cooked through, rearranging once during cooking. Remove chicken; cover to keep warm.

3 Stir blended cornflour and water into juices in dish; cook, uncovered, on HIGH (100%) about 2 minutes or until sauce boils and thickens. Return chicken to dish; coat with sauce.

4 Combine yogurt, garam masala and mint in small bowl; serve with chicken and fruity couscous.

fruity couscous Combine butter, onion and garam masala in large microwave-safe bowl; cook, uncovered, on HIGH (100%) 4 minutes, stirring once during cooking. Add currants, apricots and stock; cook, covered, on HIGH (100%) 2 minutes or until boiling. Stir in couscous; stand, covered, 5 minutes. Fluff with fork.

½ cup (125ml) honey
1 tablespoon wholegrain mustard
2 tablespoons lemon juice
2 teaspoons finely chopped fresh rosemary
6 (660g) chicken thigh fillets, halved
2 teaspoons cornflour
2 teaspoons water
200ml plain yogurt
½ teaspoon garam masala
1 tablespoon shredded fresh mint leaves
fruity couscous
20g butter
1 medium (150g) brown onion, sliced thinly
1 teaspoon garam masala
¼ cup (35g) currants
¼ cup (35g) finely chopped dried apricots
1¼ cups (310ml) hot chicken stock
1 cup (200g) couscous

- prep time: 25 minutes
- cook time: 25 minutes
- serves: 4
- per serve: 13.8g fat; 605 cal

chilli chicken & chorizo casserole

250g chorizo, sliced

1 tablespoon olive oil

9 (1.5kg) chicken thigh cutlets

1 large (300g) red onion, sliced

4 cloves garlic, crushed

2 teaspoons ground cumin

2 teaspoons sweet paprika

3 large (750g) tomatoes, chopped

½ cup (125ml) chicken stock

2 tablespoons chilli sauce

2 tablespoons chopped fresh oregano

2 tablespoons lemon juice

1 Cook chorizo between double thicknesses of absorbent paper on HIGH (100%) about 3 minutes or until crisp.

2 Combine oil, chicken, onion, garlic and spices in 3-litre shallow microwave-safe dish; cook, covered, on MEDIUM-HIGH (70%) 10 minutes, turning chicken pieces once during cooking.

3 Add chorizo, tomato, stock, sauce, oregano and juice; cook, covered, on MEDIUM-HIGH (70%) 20 minutes, turning chicken pieces once during cooking.

- prep time: 20 minutes
- cook time: 35 minutes
- serves: 6
- per serve: 134.5g fat; 501 cal

chicken satay

1 Combine peanut butter, stock, honey, soy, paste, juice and powder in large bowl with chicken. Stir to mix well, cover; refrigerate several hours or overnight.

2 Drain chicken over medium microwave-safe bowl; reserve marinade. Thread chicken onto 8 bamboo skewers.

3 Stir milk into reserved marinade; cook, uncovered, on HIGH (100%) about 5 minutes or until sauce boils and thickens slightly, stirring once during cooking.

4 Place skewers, in single layer, in large shallow microwave-safe dish; cook, uncovered, on MEDIUM-HIGH (70%) about 8 minutes or until cooked through, turning skewers once during cooking. Serve with sauce.

½ cup (130g) crunchy
   peanut butter
¼ cup (60ml) chicken stock
2 tablespoons honey
2 tablespoons soy sauce
1 tablespoon Thai red curry
   paste
1 tablespoon lemon juice
3 teaspoons mild curry
   powder
500g chicken thigh fillets,
   sliced
1 cup (250ml) coconut milk

- **prep time: 30 minutes**
  (plus marinating time)
- **cook time: 15 minutes**
- **serves: 4**
- **per serve: 38g fat; 561 cal**

chicken with soy plum sauce

¼ cup (60ml) soy sauce

2 tablespoons dry sherry

1 tablespoon plum sauce

1 tablespoon vegetable oil

2 cloves garlic, crushed

2 teaspoons grated fresh
ginger

¼ teaspoon five-spice
powder

1 tablespoon honey

1.5kg chicken

2 teaspoons cornflour

½ cup (125ml) water

1 Combine soy, sherry, plum sauce, oil, garlic, ginger, five-spice powder and honey in large bowl with chicken, cover; refrigerate overnight.

2 Drain over medium microwave-safe bowl; reserve marinade.

3 Place chicken, breast-side down, in shallow microwave-safe dish; cook, uncovered, on MEDIUM-HIGH (70%) 20 minutes.

4 Turn chicken onto back; cook, uncovered, on MEDIUM-HIGH (70%) 10 minutes. Cover ends of drumsticks and wings with small pieces of foil to prevent overcooking (do not allow foil to touch oven walls). Cook, uncovered, on MEDIUM-HIGH (70%) a further 10 minutes or until chicken is cooked through, brushing with a little marinade twice during cooking. After cooking, check the internal temperature of the chicken with a meat thermometer. The chicken must reach an internal temperature of 87°C. Stand, covered, 10 minutes.

5 Add blended cornflour and water to reserved marinade in bowl; cook, uncovered, on HIGH (100%) about 2 minutes or until sauce b oils and thickens, whisking once during cooking. Serve sauce with chicken.

- **prep time: 15 minutes (plus marinating time)**
- **cook time: 55 minutes**
- **serves: 4**
- **per serve: 32.9g fat; 499 cal**

beef & nut biryani

1 Combine beef with sambal, ground spices, vinegar and yogurt in medium bowl, cover; refrigerate 30 minutes.

2 Place rice in medium bowl, cover with water; stand 30 minutes, drain.

3 Combine ghee and onion in large microwave-safe bowl; cook, covered, on HIGH (100%) 6 minutes, stirring once during cooking.

4 Add beef mixture, rice and stock to onion mixture; cook, covered, on MEDIUM-HIGH (70%) about 20 minutes or until rice is tender and beef cooked through, stirring once during cooking.

5 Stir peas, tomato and fresh coriander into rice mixture, cover; stand 5 minutes.

6 Meanwhile, cook nuts on microwave-safe plate, uncovered, on HIGH (100%) about 3 minutes or until browned lightly, stirring twice during cooking. Stir into biryani.

500g beef fillet steak, sliced thinly
2 teaspoons sambal oelek
2 teaspoons ground coriander
1 teaspoon ground cumin
1 teaspoon ground turmeric
1 tablespoon white vinegar
⅓ cup (80ml) plain yogurt
2 cups (400g) white long-grain rice
50g ghee
2 large (400g) brown onions, chopped finely
2 cups (500ml) hot beef stock
1 cup (125g) frozen peas, thawed
2 medium (380g) tomatoes, chopped coarsely
2 tablespoons chopped fresh coriander leaves
¾ cup (105g) slivered almonds

- **prep time: 30 minutes (plus chilling and standing time)**
- **cook time: 35 minutes**
- **serves: 4**
- **per serve: 36.5g fat; 882 cal**

creamy beef stroganoff

60g butter

1 medium (150g) brown
  onion, sliced

2 cloves garlic, crushed

1 teaspoon sweet paprika

250g button mushrooms,
  sliced

500g beef fillet steak, sliced
  thinly

2 tablespoons plain flour

1 cup (250ml) beef stock

1 tablespoon dry sherry

2 tablespoons tomato paste

1 teaspoon worcestershire
  sauce

½ cup (125ml) soured cream

1 tablespoon chopped fresh
  chives

1 Combine butter, onion, garlic and paprika in large microwave-safe bowl; cook, uncovered, on HIGH (100%) 4 minutes, stirring once during cooking.

2 Add mushrooms; cook, uncovered, on HIGH (100%) 2 minutes. Coat beef with flour, add to mushroom mixture; cook, uncovered, on MEDIUM-HIGH (70%) 2 minutes.

3 Add stock, sherry, paste and sauce; cook, uncovered, on MEDIUM-HIGH (70%) about 15 minutes or until beef is tender and mixture thickens slightly, stirring twice during cooking. Stir in soured cream and chives.

- prep time: 25 minutes
- cook time: 25 minutes
- serves: 4
- per serve: 32.7g fat;
  469 cal

home-style meatloaf

1 Combine oil, onion and pepper in medium microwave-safe bowl; cook, covered, on HIGH (100%) 4 minutes, stirring once during cooking.

2 Add minced beef, sausagemeat, breadcrumbs, egg, paste and oregano to same bowl, mix well.

3 Shape mixture into a 10cm x 25cm loaf on microwave oven turntable. Brush with combined sauces and sugar; cook, uncovered, on MEDIUM (55%) about 30 minutes or until firm. Stand, covered, 10 minutes.

1 tablespoon olive oil
1 medium (150g) brown
  onion, chopped
1 small (150g) red pepper,
  chopped
500g minced beef
250g sausagemeat
1 cup (70g) stale
  breadcrumbs
1 egg
2 tablespoons tomato paste
2 teaspoons chopped fresh
  oregano
1 tablespoon tomato sauce
2 teaspoons soy sauce
2 teaspoons brown sugar

- **prep time: 15 minutes**
- **cook time: 45 minutes**
- **serves: 6**
- **per serve: 24.1g fat;
  358 cal**

lamb rogan josh

⅓ cup (90g) rogan josh curry
  paste
1 large (200g) brown onion,
  sliced
1 clove garlic, crushed
800g lamb fillets, sliced thinly
¼ cup (60ml) plain yogurt
400g can tomatoes
2 teaspoons cornflour
1 tablespoon water
1 tablespoon chopped fresh
  coriander leaves
1 tablespoon chopped fresh
  mint leaves

1 Combine paste, onion and garlic in large microwave-safe bowl; cook, covered, on HIGH (100%) 5 minutes, stirring once during cooking.

2 Stir in lamb and yogurt; cook, covered, on MEDIUM-HIGH (70%) 5 minutes, stirring once during cooking. Add undrained crushed tomatoes; cook, uncovered, on MEDIUM-HIGH (70%) 10 minutes, stirring gently once during cooking.

3 Stir in blended cornflour and water; cook, uncovered, on MEDIUM-HIGH (70%) about 2 minutes or until mixture boils and thickens slightly. Stir in herbs.

- **prep time: 20 minutes**
- **cook time: 25 minutes**
- **serves: 6**
- **per serve: 16.6g fat;
  301 cal**

chilli garlic lamb with noodles

1 Combine lamb with chilli and hoisin sauce, sherry and garlic in large microwave-safe bowl, cover; refrigerate 3 hours or overnight.

2 Rinse noodles in hot water to separate; drain.

3 Stir oil into undrained lamb mixture; cook, uncovered, on MEDIUM-HIGH (70%) 8 minutes, stirring once during cooking.

4 Add broccoli, soy sauce, peanut butter and blended cornflour and the water; cook, uncovered, on MEDIUM-HIGH (70%) about 4 minutes or until mixture boils and thickens slightly.

5 Toss noodles through lamb mixture; cook, uncovered, on MEDIUM-HIGH (70%) about 3 minutes or until hot.

500g lamb fillets, sliced
2 tablespoons mild chilli sauce
2 tablespoons hoisin sauce
2 tablespoons sweet sherry
2 cloves garlic, crushed
500g thick fresh egg noodles
2 tablespoons groundnut oil
1 bunch gai lan (chinese broccoli), chopped coarsely
2 tablespoons soy sauce
2 teaspoons smooth peanut butter
2 teaspoons cornflour
½ cup (125ml) water

prep time: 25 minutes (plus marinating time)
cook time: 20 minutes
serves: 4
per serve: 23.1g fat; 520 cal

quick lamb curry with mango relish

¼ cup (65g) Madras curry
   paste
1 medium (150g) brown
   onion, sliced
1 tablespoon grated
   fresh ginger
2 cloves garlic, crushed
480g lamb fillets, sliced thinly
⅓ cup (80ml) plain yogurt
2 teaspoons cornflour
½ cup (125ml) beef stock
1 tablespoon chopped fresh
   coriander leaves

mango relish

1 medium (430g) mango,
   chopped coarsely
1 tablespoon chopped fresh
   coriander leaves
2 teaspoons white wine
   vinegar
½ teaspoon sweet chilli
   sauce

1 Combine paste, onion, ginger and garlic in large microwave-safe bowl; cook, covered, on HIGH (100%) 4 minutes, stirring once during cooking.

2 Add lamb; cook, covered, on MEDIUM-HIGH (70%) about 5 minutes or until lamb is just cooked, stirring once during cooking.

3 Stir in yogurt, blended cornflour and stock; cook, uncovered, on MEDIUM-HIGH (70%) about 5 minutes or until mixture boils and thickens slightly, stirring twice during cooking. Stir in coriander. Serve with mango relish.

mango relish Combine all relish ingredients in medium bowl, cover; refrigerate until required.

- prep time: 25 minutes
- cook time: 15 minutes
- serves: 4
- per serve: 19.1g fat;
  355 cal

mustard lamb racks with sun-dried tomato crust

1 Spread backs of lamb racks with mustard. Combine breadcrumbs, garlic, tomato and egg white in small bowl, press onto mustard.

2 Place lamb racks, crust-side up, with meaty ends towards edge of large shallow microwave-safe dish; cook, uncovered, on MEDIUM-HIGH (70%) about 12 minutes or until almost cooked as desired. Stand, covered, 10 minutes. Serve with fresh thyme sauce.

fresh thyme sauce Blend cornflour with the water in microwave-safe jug, stir in stock, wine and juice; cook, uncovered, on HIGH (100%) about 3 minutes or until sauce boils and thickens slightly, whisking once during cooking. Stir in tomato and thyme.

4 racks of lamb with 4 cutlets each
1 tablespoon dijon mustard
1 cup (70g) stale breadcrumbs
2 cloves garlic, crushed
¼ cup (35g) drained finely chopped sun-dried tomatoes in oil
1 egg white, beaten lightly
fresh thyme sauce
3 teaspoons cornflour
1 tablespoon water
½ cup (125ml) beef stock
1 tablespoon dry red wine
½ cup (125ml) tomato juice
1 tablespoon drained finely chopped sun-dried tomatoes in oil
1 teaspoon chopped fresh thyme

prep time: 15 minutes
cook time: 25 minutes
serves: 4
per serve: 30g fat; 476 cal

pork with caramelised apples

800g pork fillets

2 teaspoons cornflour

1 tablespoon water

⅓ cup (80ml) orange juice

¼ cup (60ml) chicken stock

2 tablespoons port

2 tablespoons blackberry
  jam

20g butter

2 medium (300g) red apples,
  sliced

2 tablespoons brown sugar

1 Cook pork in large shallow microwave-safe dish, uncovered, on MEDIUM (55%) 5 minutes; drain. Turn pork; cook, uncovered, on MEDIUM (55%) 5 minutes. Repeat once more or until pork is almost tender; cover, stand 5 minutes.

2 Blend cornflour with water in microwave-safe jug, stir in juice, stock, port and jam; cook, uncovered, on HIGH (100%) **for** about 2 minutes or until sauce boils and thickens, whisking once during cooking.

3 Melt butter in large shallow microwave-safe dish, uncovered, on HIGH (100%) 30 seconds. Stir in apple and sugar, cook, uncovered, on HIGH (100%) about 5 minutes or until apples are soft, stirring once during cooking. Serve pork with apples and sauce.

prep time: 20 minutes

cook time: 30 minutes

serves: 6

per serve: 4.9g fat;
249 cal

satay pork noodles

1 Combine oil, pork, onion and garlic in large shallow microwave-safe dish; cook, uncovered, on MEDIUM-HIGH (70%) about 10 minutes or until pork is just cooked. Drain.

2 Add peanut butter, sauce, milk, stock, juice, sugar and coriander; cook, uncovered, on MEDIUM-HIGH (70%) about 4 minutes or until hot.

3 Rinse noodles in hot water to separate; drain. Toss chives and noodles through pork mixture in dish; cook, uncovered, on MEDIUM-HIGH (70%) about 3 minutes or until hot.

2 tablespoons groundnut oil
750g pork fillet, sliced thinly
1 medium (150g) brown onion, sliced
1 clove garlic, crushed
½ cup (130g) smooth peanut butter
¼ cup (60ml) sweet chilli sauce
⅔ cup (160ml) coconut milk
¾ cup (180ml) chicken stock
2 tablespoons lime juice
1 teaspoon sugar
1 tablespoon chopped fresh coriander leaves
450g fresh chow mein noodles
50g garlic chives, halved

- prep time: 25 minutes
- cook time: 20 minutes
- serves: 4
- per serve: 41.4g fat; 765 cal

risotto marinara

30 (750g) medium uncooked
   prawns
2 tablespoons olive oil
1 medium (150g) brown
   onion, chopped finely
2 cups (400g) arborio rice
3½ cups (875ml) hot
   vegetable stock
500g seafood marinara mix
½ cup (125ml) double cream
½ cup (40g) coarsely grated
   parmesan cheese
¼ cup chopped fresh flat-leaf
   parsley

1 Shell and devein prawns, cut in half lengthways.
2 Combine oil and onion in large microwave-safe bowl;
cook, uncovered, on HIGH (100%) 4 minutes, stirring once
during cooking. Stir in rice; cook, uncovered, on HIGH (100%)
1 minute.
3 Add stock; cook, covered, on HIGH (100%) 10 minutes,
stirring twice during cooking.
4 Stir in all seafood; cook, covered, on MEDIUM (55%) about
6 minutes or until seafood has changed in colour and rice is
just tender, stirring once during cooking.
5 Stir in cream and cheese; cook, covered, on MEDIUM (55%)
3 minutes. Stand, covered, 5 minutes; stir in parsley.

- **prep time: 30 minutes**
- **cook time: 30 minutes**
- **serves: 4**
- **per serve: 30.2g fat;**
  821 cal

salmon & pasta mornay

1 Combine pasta with the boiling water in large microwave-safe bowl; cook, uncovered, on HIGH (100%) about 12 minutes or until just tender, stirring twice during cooking. Drain pasta; place in 2-litre shallow microwave-safe dish.

2 Cook broccoli in large microwave-safe bowl, uncovered, on HIGH (100%) 3 minutes, rinse under cold water; drain. Place broccoli, flaked salmon and onion with pasta in dish.

3 Melt butter in large microwave-safe bowl, uncovered, on HIGH (100%) 30 seconds. Whisk in flour; cook, uncovered, on HIGH (100%) 30 seconds. Whisk in milk and cream; cook, uncovered, on HIGH (100%) about 5 minutes or until sauce boils and thickens, whisking twice during cooking. Whisk in rind, mustard and cheese.

4 Pour sauce over pasta mixture, sprinkle with paprika; cook, uncovered, on MEDIUM (55%) about 10 minutes or until hot.

200g pasta shapes
1.5 litres boiling water
400g broccoli, chopped
415g can red salmon, drained
3 spring onions, chopped
30g butter
⅓ cup (50g) plain flour
2 cups (500ml) milk
⅓ cup (80ml) double cream
½ teaspoon finely grated lemon rind
2 teaspoons wholegrain mustard
½ cup (60g) coarsely grated cheddar cheese
½ teaspoon sweet paprika

- prep time: 25 minutes
- cook time: 30 minutes
- serves: 4
- per serve: 34.7g fat; 673 cal

cajun fish fillets with tabasco butter

¼ cup (30g) sweet paprika
¼ cup (40g) cracked black
   pepper
1 teaspoon cayenne pepper
2 cloves garlic, crushed
¼ cup chopped fresh thyme
4 medium (800g) white fish
   fillets
60g butter
1 teaspoon Tabasco sauce

1 Combine paprika, peppers, garlic and thyme in small bowl; coat fish with pepper mixture.
2 Cook fish in large shallow microwave-safe dish, covered, on MEDIUM (55%) about 10 minutes or until cooked as desired; drain.
3 Heat butter and sauce in small microwave-safe bowl, uncovered, on HIGH (100%) about 1 minute; pour over fish.

- prep time: 15 minutes
- cook time: 10 minutes
- serves: 4
- per serve: 17.9g fat; 331 cal

tomato garlic prawns

1 Shell and devein prawns, leaving tails intact.

2 Combine oil, butter, onion and garlic in large microwave-safe bowl; cook, covered, on HIGH (100%) 4 minutes, stirring once during cooking.

3 Add wine, tomato, paste, sugar, and half the parsley; cook, uncovered, on HIGH (100%) about 15 minutes or until mixture thickens, stirring once during cooking.

4 Add prawns; cook, covered, on MEDIUM (55%) about 10 minutes or until prawns change in colour, stirring once during cooking. Serve sprinkled with remaining parsley.

40 (1kg) medium uncooked prawns
2 tablespoons olive oil
50g butter
1 medium (170g) red onion, chopped finely
3 cloves garlic, crushed
2 tablespoons dry red wine
3 large (750g) tomatoes, peeled, chopped
2 tablespoons tomato paste
½ teaspoon sugar
2 tablespoons chopped fresh flat-leaf parsley

- prep time: 40 minutes
- cook time: 30 minutes
- serves: 4
- per serve: 20.8g fat; 338 cal

singapore noodles

10 dried shiitake mushrooms

450g thin fresh egg noodles

16 (400g) medium uncooked
  prawns

2 tablespoons groundnut oil

5 cloves garlic, crushed

1 tablespoon grated
  fresh ginger

2 tablespoons mild curry
  paste

230g can water chestnuts,
  drained, chopped

4 spring onions, chopped

200g Chinese barbecued
  pork, sliced

2 tablespoons soy sauce

2 tablespoons oyster sauce

2 tablespoons dry sherry

3 eggs, beaten lightly

2 teaspoons sesame oil

1 Place mushrooms in small heatproof bowl, cover with boiling water, stand 20 minutes; drain. Discard stems; chop mushroom caps finely.

2 Rinse noodles under cold water; drain. Shell and devein prawns, leaving tails intact.

3 Combine oil, garlic, ginger and paste in large microwave-safe bowl; cook, covered, on HIGH (100%) 1 minute. Add mushrooms, chestnuts, onion and pork; cook, uncovered, on MEDIUM-HIGH (70%) 2 minutes.

4 Add prawns; cook, uncovered, on MEDIUM (55%) about 5 minutes or until prawns just change in colour. Add noodles, combined sauces and sherry; cook, uncovered, on MEDIUM (55%) 4 minutes, stirring once during cooking.

5 Add combined eggs and sesame oil; mix gently. Cook, uncovered, on MEDIUM (55%) about 3 minutes or until eggs are just cooked, stirring gently once during cooking.

**prep time: 35 minutes
(plus standing time)**

cook time: 15 minutes

serves: 4

per serve: 30g fat; 578 cal

curried vegetable & bacon patties

1 Combine potato with the water in large microwave-safe bowl; cook, covered, on HIGH (100%) about 10 minutes or until tender; drain.

2 Mash potato, butter, cream and egg yolk together in same bowl.

3 Combine bacon, onion and garlic in large microwave-safe bowl; cook, covered, on HIGH (100%) 4 minutes, stirring once during cooking.

4 Stir in curry powder and vegetables; cook, covered, on HIGH (100%) 2 minutes. Stir in potato mixture and stale breadcrumbs, cover; refrigerate 1 hour.

5 Shape mixture into 8 patties, press corn flake crumbs all over patties. Place patties around edge of microwave oven turntable; cook, uncovered, on HIGH (100%) 5 minutes.

4 medium (800g) potatoes, chopped coarsely
2 tablespoons water
30g butter
2 tablespoons double cream
1 egg yolk
6 bacon rashers, chopped
1 small (80g) brown onion, chopped finely
1 clove garlic, crushed
1 tablespoon mild curry powder
2 cups (160g) shredded cabbage
1 medium (120g) carrot, grated coarsely
3 cups (210g) stale breadcrumbs
½ cup (75g) corn flakes, crushed into crumbs

- prep time: 30 minutes (plus chilling time)
- cook time: 25 minutes
- serves: 4
- per serve: 24.6g fat; 584 cal

chickpea & vegetable stuffed peppers

3 medium (600g) red peppers

2 medium (240g) courgettes, chopped finely

1 small (80g) brown onion, sliced thinly

100g green beans, chopped

300g can chickpeas, rinsed, drained

1 tablespoon olive oil

½ cup (40g) flaked parmesan cheese

tomato sauce

2 x 400g cans tomatoes

1 tablespoon balsamic vinegar

½ teaspoon sugar

¼ cup shredded fresh basil leaves

1 Halve peppers lengthways, remove seeds and membranes. Place pepper halves, cut-side up, in 3-litre shallow microwave-safe dish.

2 Spoon combined courgette, onion, beans, chickpeas and oil into pepper halves; pour over tomato sauce. Cook, covered, on HIGH (100%) about 20 minutes or until vegetables are tender. Serve topped with cheese.

tomato sauce Combine undrained crushed tomatoes, vinegar and sugar in large microwave-safe bowl; cook, uncovered, on HIGH (100%) 8 minutes, stirring once during cooking. Stir in basil.

- prep time: 20 minutes
- cook time: 30 minutes
- serves: 6
- per serve: 6.5g fat; 145 cal

ratatouille casserole

1 Combine oil, garlic and leek in 3-litre shallow microwave-safe dish; cook, uncovered, on HIGH (100%) 4 minutes, stirring once during cooking.

2 Add aubergine, peppers, courgettes, mushrooms and wine; cook, covered, on HIGH (100%) 5 minutes.

3 Add undrained crushed tomatoes, puree, beans, sugar and oregano; cook, uncovered, on HIGH (100%) 15 minutes, stirring twice during cooking.

4 Place polenta squares on top of mixture; sprinkle with cheese. Cook, uncovered, on MEDIUM (55%) about 10 minutes.

lentil polenta topping Combine lentils with the boiling water in large microwave-safe bowl; cook, uncovered, on HIGH (100%) 10 minutes, stirring once during cooking. Drain; cool. Combine milk, hot stock and the hot water in large microwave-safe bowl, stir in polenta; cook, uncovered, on HIGH (100%) about 8 minutes or until mixture thickens, stirring every 2 minutes. Stir in lentils, cheese and parsley. Using a damp spatula, press mixture into oiled 26cm x 32cm swiss roll tin; cool. Cover and refrigerate until cold. Turn onto board and cut into 5cm squares.

1 tablespoon olive oil
1 clove garlic, crushed
1 small (200g) leek, chopped
1 small (230g) aubergine, chopped coarsely
2 medium (400g) green peppers, chopped
2 medium (400g) red peppers, chopped
2 medium (240g) courgettes, sliced thickly
200g mushrooms, halved
¼ cup (60ml) dry white wine
400g can tomatoes
½ cup (125ml) tomato puree
200g green beans, halved
2 teaspoons sugar
1 tablespoon chopped fresh oregano
2 tablespoons finely grated parmesan cheese

lentil polenta topping
½ cup (100g) red lentils
2 cups (500ml) boiling water
1 cup (250ml) milk
1½ cups (375ml) hot vegetable stock
1½ cups (375ml) hot water
1 cup (170g) polenta
½ cup (40g) finely grated parmesan cheese
1 tablespoon finely chopped fresh flat-leaf parsley

- prep time: 40 minutes (plus refrigeration time)
- cook time: 50 minutes
- serves: 6
- per serve: 9.7g fat; 326 cal
- tip: the lentil polenta topping can be made the day before and kept, covered, in the refrigerator.

potato frittata

2 teaspoons vegetable oil

1 large (200g) brown onion, sliced thinly

1 clove garlic, crushed

1 small (150g) red pepper, chopped finely

130g can corn kernels, drained

2 teaspoons chopped fresh oregano

2 medium (400g) potatoes, sliced thinly

6 eggs, beaten lightly

½ cup (125ml) milk

2 teaspoons chopped fresh thyme

½ cup (60g) coarsely grated cheddar cheese

1 Grease 20cm-square 2-litre microwave-safe dish; line base with baking parchment, extending paper 2cm above two opposite sides of dish.

2 Combine oil, onion, garlic and pepper in medium microwave-safe bowl; cook, covered, on HIGH (100%) 3 minutes, stirring once during cooking. Drain on kitchen paper; combine mixture with corn and oregano in same bowl.

3 Layer half the potato over base of prepared dish, top with onion mixture then remaining potato. Pour over combined eggs and milk; cook, uncovered, on MEDIUM (55%) about 20 minutes or until centre is almost set.

4 Sprinkle with thyme and cheese; cook, uncovered, on MEDIUM (55%) about 8 minutes or until cheese melts and frittata is just set. Stand, covered, 5 minutes.

prep time: 30 minutes

cook time: 35 minutes

serves: 4

per serve: 17.7g fat; 316 cal

curried chickpeas & rice

1 Combine rice with the boiling water in large microwave-safe bowl; cook uncovered, on HIGH (100%) about 25 minutes or until tender. Drain.

2 Combine paste, onion and garlic in large microwave-safe bowl; cook, covered, on HIGH (100%) 5 minutes, stirring once during cooking. Add chickpeas and stock; cook, covered, on HIGH (100%) 10 minutes.

3 Stir in chutney, cream and rice; cook, uncovered, on HIGH (100%) 5 minutes. Stir in fresh coriander leaves.

⅔ cup (130g) brown long-grain rice
1.5 litres boiling water
2 tablespoons mild curry paste
2 medium (300g) brown onions, chopped finely
2 cloves garlic, crushed
2 x 425g cans chickpeas, rinsed, drained
1½ cups (375ml) hot chicken stock
1 tablespoon mango chutney
1 cup (250ml) coconut cream
¼ cup finely chopped fresh coriander leaves

- prep time: 15 minutes
- cook time: 45 minutes
- serves: 4
- per serve: 21.3g fat; 453 cal

vegetable & split pea curry

1 cup (200g) green split peas
1 tablespoon groundnut oil
1 large (200g) brown onion, sliced
1 tablespoon mild curry powder
2 teaspoons ground ginger
2 teaspoons ground cumin
2 teaspoons ground coriander
1 teaspoon ground turmeric
400g can tomatoes
¾ cup (180ml) vegetable stock
1 cup (250ml) coconut milk
10 (400g) tiny new potatoes, quartered
1 medium (400g) sweet potato, chopped
2 medium (240g) carrots, chopped
4 medium (480g) courgettes, chopped
1 tablespoon chopped fresh coriander leaves
1 tablespoon lime juice

1 Place peas in medium bowl, cover with cold water, soak 1 hour; drain.

2 Combine oil, onion, powder and ground spices in 3-litre shallow microwave-safe dish; cook, covered, on HIGH (100%) 5 minutes, stirring gently once during cooking.

3 Add peas, undrained crushed tomatoes and stock; cook, covered, on HIGH (100%) 15 minutes.

4 Add milk and vegetables; cook, covered, on HIGH (100%) about 20 minutes or until vegetables and peas are tender, stirring gently twice during cooking. Stir in fresh coriander and juice.

- **prep time: 25 minutes (plus soaking time)**
- **cook time: 40 minutes**
- **serves: 6**
- **per serve: 14.8g fat; 355 cal**

risotto primavera

1 Cook asparagus in large microwave-safe bowl, covered, on HIGH (100%) 1 minute. Rinse asparagus under cold water; drain.

2 Combine oil, rice and garlic in same bowl; cook, covered, on HIGH (100%) 1 minute. Add 2 cups (500ml) of the stock; cook, covered, on HIGH (100%) 5 minutes. Stir then add remaining stock; cook, covered, on HIGH (100%) 5 minutes, stirring once during cooking.

3 Stir peas, cream, mustard and cheese into risotto; cook, covered, on MEDIUM (55%) 5 minutes. Stand, covered, 5 minutes. Stir in asparagus and mint.

250g fresh asparagus, trimmed, chopped
2 tablespoons olive oil
1½ cups (300g) arborio rice
1 clove garlic, crushed
1 litre hot chicken stock
1 cup (125g) frozen peas
¼ cup (60ml) double cream
2 teaspoons dijon mustard
⅓ cup (25g) coarsely grated parmesan cheese
2 tablespoons finely chopped fresh mint leaves

- prep time: 15 minutes
- cook time: 25 minutes
- serves: 4
- per serve: 19g fat; 511 cal

vegetarian nachos

2 teaspoons olive oil
1 medium (150g) brown
  onion, chopped finely
2 cloves garlic, crushed
¼ cup (60ml) tomato paste
1 teaspoon ground cumin
450g can refried beans
425g can mixed beans in
  spicy sauce
1 medium (250g) avocado
2 teaspoons lime juice
1 teaspoon Tabasco sauce
250g plain corn chips
1 cup (125g) coarsely grated
  cheddar cheese
½ cup (125ml) soured cream
½ cup (125ml) bottled salsa

1 Combine oil, onion and garlic in large microwave-safe bowl; cook, uncovered, on HIGH (100%) 4 minutes, stirring once during cooking. Add paste, cumin, refried beans and undrained beans; cook, uncovered, on HIGH (100%) 3 minutes.

2 Mash avocado with fork in small bowl; stir in juice and sauce. Cover tightly; refrigerate until required.

3 Divide corn chips among 4 microwave-safe plates. Spoon equal amounts of bean mixture in centre of chips, sprinkle with cheese; cook, 1 plate at a time, uncovered, on MEDIUM (55%) about 2 minutes or until cheese melts. Top Nachos with soured cream, salsa and avocado.

- prep time: 25 minutes
- cook time: 15 minutes
- serves: 4
- per serve: 51.3g fat; 855 cal
- tip: mexe-Beans are a canned pinto-bean mixture containing chilli, garlic, onion and various spices.

crustless courgette quiche

1 Oil shallow 24cm-round, 1.5-litre microwave-safe dish.
2 Combine courgette, cheddar cheese, onion, flour, garlic, parsley, milk, cream and eggs in large bowl; mix well. Pour mixture into prepared dish, top with tomato and olives; sprinkle with parmesan cheese.
3 Cook, uncovered, on MEDIUM (55%) about 20 minutes or until centre is almost set. Stand, covered, 15 minutes.

1 large (150g) courgette, grated coarsely
1½ cups (185g) coarsely grated cheddar cheese
3 spring onions, chopped
⅓ cup (50g) plain flour
1 clove garlic, crushed
1 tablespoon finely chopped fresh parsley
1 cup (250ml) milk
½ cup (125ml) soured cream
4 eggs, beaten lightly
2 medium (150g) egg tomatoes, sliced
⅓ cup (40g) pitted black olives
1 tablespoon finely grated parmesan cheese

- prep time: 20 minutes
- cook time: 35 minutes
- serves: 4
- per serve: 39.4g fat; 503 cal

creamy broccoli & bacon pasta

500g fresh fettuccine
1.5 litres boiling water
30g butter
1 small (80g) brown onion,
 chopped
2 bacon rashers, chopped
1 clove garlic, crushed
250g broccoli, chopped
 finely
2 teaspoons cornflour
1 tablespoon water, extra
1 chicken stock cube
300ml double cream
2 tablespoons finely grated
 parmesan cheese

1 Combine pasta with the boiling water in large microwave-safe bowl; cook, uncovered, on HIGH (100%) about 5 minutes or until pasta is tender, stirring once during cooking. Drain pasta; cover to keep warm.

2 Combine butter, onion, bacon and garlic in large microwave-safe bowl; cook, uncovered, on HIGH (100%) 4 minutes, stirring once during cooking. Add broccoli; cook, covered, on HIGH (100%) 2 minutes.

3 Stir in blended cornflour and the extra water, crumbled stock cube, cream and cheese; cook, uncovered, on HIGH (100%) about 3 minutes or until sauce boils and thickens slightly, stirring once during cooking. Toss pasta through hot sauce.

prep time: 20 minutes
cook time: 15 minutes
serves: 4
per serve: 47g fat; 829 cal

chicken & mushroom lasagne

1 Place lasagne in large heatproof dish, cover with boiling water; stand 5 minutes, drain, pat dry with kitchen paper.

2 Cook onion in large microwave-safe bowl, uncovered, on HIGH (100%) 3 minutes. Add mushrooms; cook, uncovered, on HIGH (100%) 4 minutes, stirring once during cooking. Drain excess liquid away, then stir in wine, chicken and oregano.

3 Melt butter in large microwave-safe bowl, uncovered, on HIGH (100%) 30 seconds. Whisk in flour; cook, uncovered, on HIGH (100%) 30 seconds. Whisk in milk; cook, uncovered on HIGH (100%) 5 minutes until sauce boils and thickens, whisking twice during cooking. Whisk in mustard and half the cheese.

4 Line base of 18cm x 28cm 2-litre microwave-safe dish with 2 lasagne sheets. Top with a third of the sauce, half the chicken mixture then 3 lasagne sheets. Repeat, ending with a layer of sauce. Cook, uncovered, on MEDIUM (55%) 12 minutes.

5 Sprinkle with remaining cheese. Shield corners of dish with 6cm x 12cm strips of foil (do not allow foil to touch oven walls). Cook, uncovered, on MEDIUM (55%) about 10 minutes or until pasta is tender. Stand, covered, 10 minutes.

8 quick-cook lasagne sheets
2 medium (300g) brown
  onions, chopped
500g flat mushrooms, sliced
  finely
½ cup (125ml) dry white wine
2 cups (340g) chopped
  cooked chicken
2 tablespoons chopped fresh
  oregano
45g butter
⅓ cup (50g) plain flour
2 cups (500ml) milk
1 tablespoon wholegrain
  mustard
1½ cups (185g) coarsely
  grated cheddar cheese

- prep time: 40 minutes
- cook time: 45 minutes
- serves: 4
- per serve: 38.4g fat;
  728 cal

macaroni cheese

300g macaroni
2 litres boiling water
2 bacon rashers, chopped
  finely
60g butter
½ cup (75g) plain flour
2½ cups (625ml) milk
½ cup (125ml) double cream
pinch ground nutmeg
1 teaspoon dijon mustard
1½ cups (185g) coarsely
  grated cheddar cheese
½ cup (40g) coarsely grated
  parmesan cheese
½ cup (35g) stale
  breadcrumbs
1 tablespoon chopped fresh
  chives

1 Combine the pasta with the boiling water in large microwave-safe bowl; cook, uncovered, on HIGH (100%) about 12 minutes or until pasta is just tender. Drain.
2 Place bacon in large microwave-safe bowl, cover with sheet of absorbent paper; cook on HIGH (100%) 3 minutes. Discard absorbent paper; add butter, stir until melted.
3 Whisk in flour; cook, uncovered, on HIGH (100%) 1 minute. Whisk in milk and cream; cook, uncovered, on HIGH (100%) about 6 minutes or until sauce boils and thickens, whisking twice during cooking.
4 Add nutmeg, mustard and half the combined cheeses, stir until cheeses melt; add pasta, mix well.
5 Spoon pasta mixture into oiled 2-litre shallow microwave-safe dish. Top with breadcrumbs, remaining cheeses and chives; cook, uncovered, on MEDIUM (55%) about 15 minutes or until hot.

prep time: 20 minutes
cook time: 35 minutes
serves: 4
per serve: 55.5g fat;
959 cal

pasta carbonara

1 Break pasta in half. Combine pasta, boiling water and oil in large microwave-safe bowl; cook, uncovered, on HIGH (100%) about 12 minutes or until just tender, stirring twice during cooking. Drain pasta; cover to keep warm.

2 Place bacon in large microwave-safe bowl, cover with sheet of absorbent paper; cook on HIGH (100%) about 6 minutes or until crisp, stirring once during cooking. Discard absorbent paper. Add cream to bowl; cook, uncovered, on HIGH (100%) 4 minutes.

3 Working quickly, gently mix hot pasta and combined eggs and cheese with bacon mixture in bowl. Cook, uncovered, on MEDIUM (55%) about 2 minutes or until hot, mixing gently once during cooking.

500g fettuccine pasta
2 litres boiling water
1 teaspoon olive oil
6 bacon rashers, sliced thinly
300ml double cream
4 eggs, beaten lightly
1 cup (80g) finely grated
   parmesan cheese

- prep time: 15 minutes
- cook time: 25 minutes
- serves: 4
- per serve: 57.1g fat;
  1032 cal

Side dishes

sweet chilli, sweet potato & bean toss

1 medium (400g) sweet
  potato
300g green beans
2 tablespoons water
1 tablespoon honey
1 tablespoon sweet chilli
  sauce
1 teaspoon grated fresh
  ginger
60g butter

1 Cut sweet potato in half lengthways; cut into 1cm-thick slices. Cut beans into 5cm lengths.

2 Cook sweet potato and the water in large microwave-safe bowl, covered, on HIGH (100%) 3 minutes. Add beans; cook, covered, on HIGH (100%) 5 minutes. Drain; cover vegetables to keep warm.

3 Combine remaining ingredients in small microwave-safe bowl; cook, uncovered, on HIGH (100%) about 1 minute or until butter has melted.

4 Gently toss butter mixture through hot sweet potato and beans.

- prep time: 10 minutes
- cook time: 10 minutes
- serves: 4
- per serve: 12.7g fat; 205 cal

Cook's tip

This is an invaluable tip for any cook who has ever wrestled with a tough pumpkin or butternut squash, attempting to cut and peel it to use in soup or as a vegetable. Struggle no more! Just place a 500g piece of pumpkin on the turntable; cook, uncovered, on HIGH (100%) for 2 minutes. You won't believe how easy it is to chop.

cheese & chive potatoes

4 medium (800g) floury
potatoes, such as King
Edward or Maris Piper
1 cup (125g) coarsely grated
cheddar cheese
1 clove garlic, crushed
1 small (100g) red onion,
chopped finely
1 tablespoon finely chopped
fresh chives

1 Prick skin of potatoes in several places; place on absorbent paper around edge of microwave oven turntable. Cook potatoes, uncovered, on HIGH (100%) about 12 minutes or until tender. Stand 5 minutes before cutting off a third from top of each potato.

2 Scoop out flesh from potatoes and tops, leaving 1cm-thick shells; discard skins from tops.

3 Combine mashed potato flesh in medium bowl with cheese, garlic and onion; mix well.

4 Spoon potato mixture into potato shells, place on absorbent paper around edge of microwave turntable; cook, uncovered, on MEDIUM (55%) about 5 minutes or until hot. Sprinkle with chives.

- prep time: 25 minutes
- cook time: 25 minutes
- serves: 4
- per serve: 10.8g fat;
  263 cal

bacon & cheese potatoes

1 Prick potatoes all over with fork. Cook potatoes, in single layer, with the water in shallow microwave-safe dish, covered, on HIGH (100%) about 10 minutes or until tender, rearranging potatoes once during cooking; drain.

2 Sprinkle potatoes with cheese and bacon in dish; pour over combined cream and garlic. Cook, uncovered, on MEDIUM (55%) 5 minutes.

3 Sprinkle potatoes with parsley before serving.

16 (640g) baby new potatoes
2 tablespoons water
¼ cup (20g) finely grated parmesan cheese
2 bacon rashers, chopped finely
¼ cup (60ml) double cream
1 clove garlic, crushed
1 tablespoon chopped fresh flat-leaf parsley

- prep time: 15 minutes
- cook time: 15 minutes
- serves: 4
- per serve: 11.8g fat; 228 cal

potato & bacon casserole

4 bacon rashers, chopped
750g baby new potatoes,
 unpeeled, sliced thinly
1 medium (150g) brown
 onion, sliced thinly
½ x 40g packet salt-reduced
 chicken noodle soup mix
1 cup (250ml) double cream
1 cup (125g) coarsely grated
 cheddar cheese

1 Cook bacon between double thicknesses of absorbent paper, (see page 11) on HIGH (100%) about 5 minutes or until crisp.

2 Place potato slices in 1.5-litre shallow microwave-safe dish; cook, covered, on HIGH (100%) 5 minutes.

3 Sprinkle onion, bacon and dry soup mix over potato in dish; pour over cream. Cook, covered, on MEDIUM (55%) about 15 minutes or until potato is tender.

4 Sprinkle potato with cheese; cook, uncovered, on MEDIUM (55%) about 2 minutes or until cheese melts.

- **prep time: 15 minutes**
- **cook time: 30 minutes**
- **serves: 6**
- **per serve: 30g fat; 406 cal**

corn cobs with herb & bacon butter

1 Rinse corn under cold water; wrap each cob in microwave-safe cling film.

2 Place corn around edge of microwave turntable; cook on HIGH (100%) 10 minutes, turning corn once during cooking. Cut corn into 4cm pieces; cover to keep warm.

3 Combine bacon, onion and sambal in small microwave-safe bowl; cook, covered, on HIGH (100%) 2 minutes, stirring once during cooking. Drain bacon mixture on absorbent paper.

4 Melt butter in same small bowl on HIGH (100%) 30 seconds; add bacon mixture and herbs. Serve corn with bacon butter.

4 (1kg) corn cobs, trimmed
1 bacon rasher, chopped
1 spring onion, chopped
½ teaspoon sambal oelek
60g butter, melted
2 teaspoons chopped fresh
  flat-leaf parsley
1 teaspoon chopped fresh
  basil leaves
1 teaspoon chopped fresh
  thyme

- prep time: 15 minutes
- cook time: 15 minutes
- serves: 4
- per serve: 16.3g fat;
  301 cal

greek-style mangetout

200g mangetout, trimmed

30g butter

1 medium (150g) brown
  onion, sliced thinly

1 clove garlic, crushed

3 small (400g) tomatoes,
  chopped

1 teaspoon chopped fresh
  thyme

½ cup (60g) black olives,
  pitted

150g feta cheese, crumbled

1 Rinse mangetout under cold water; cook in shallow microwave-safe dish, covered, on HIGH (100%) 1 minute. Drain.
2 Combine butter, onion and garlic in same dish; cook, uncovered, on HIGH (100%) 4 minutes, stirring once during cooking.
3 Stir in tomato and thyme; cook, covered, on HIGH (100%) 2 minutes.
4 Stir in mangetout, olives and cheese.

- prep time: 20 minutes
- cook time: 10 minutes
- serves: 6
- per serve: 12.2g fat;
  145 cal

warm pepper salad

1 Cook nuts in small microwave-safe bowl, uncovered, on HIGH (100%) about 3 minutes or until browned lightly, stirring twice during cooking.

2 Combine onion, peppers, oil and garlic in large microwave-safe bowl; cook, covered, on HIGH (100%) about 8 minutes or until pepper is tender, stirring once during cooking. Stand 2 minutes before stirring in vinegar and nuts.

2 tablespoons pine nuts

1 small (80g) brown onion, sliced

1 medium (200g) red pepper, sliced thickly

1 medium (200g) yellow pepper, sliced thickly

1 medium (200g) green pepper, sliced thickly

2 tablespoons extra virgin olive oil

1 clove garlic, crushed

2 teaspoons balsamic vinegar

- prep time: 15 minutes
- cook time: 15 minutes
- serves: 4
- per serve: 14.4g fat; 160 cal

cheese & basil courgettes

6 medium (720g) courgettes,
  halved lengthways
3 bacon rashers, chopped
  finely
1½ tablespoons chopped
  fresh basil leaves
¾ cup (60g) finely grated
  parmesan cheese
½ cup (35g) stale
  breadcrumbs

1 Place courgettes on large microwave-safe plate with thick ends toward edge of plate. Cover, cook on HIGH (100%) about 6 minutes or until tender.

2 Scoop out flesh from courgettes, leaving 1cm-thick shell. Chop courgette flesh; combine with remaining ingredients in small bowl.

3 Spoon filling mixture into courgette shells, cover; cook on MEDIUM (55%) about 6 minutes or until just heated through.

- prep time: 15 minutes
- cook time: 15 minutes
- serves: 6
- per serve: 7.3g fat; 120 cal

layered aubergine & tomato

1 Cut aubergines into 1cm-thick slices. Place slices in colander, sprinkle with salt; stand 30 minutes. Rinse slices under cold water; drain, pat dry with absorbent paper.

2 Overlap aubergine slices in 1.5-litre shallow microwave-safe dish; cook, covered, on HIGH (100%) about 5 minutes or until tender, turning aubergines once during cooking. Drain on absorbent paper.

3 Place half of the aubergines over base of same dish, overlapping slices if necessary. Top with half of the tomato and half of the combined herbs, pepper and cheese. Repeat layers with remaining aubergine, tomato and herb mixture.

4 Cook, uncovered, on MEDIUM (55%) about 10 minutes or until cheese melts and vegetables are hot.

2 medium (600g) aubergines
coarse cooking salt
3 large (750g) tomatoes,
　peeled, sliced thickly
1 tablespoon chopped
　fresh basil leaves
1 tablespoon chopped
　fresh oregano
½ teaspoon seasoned
　pepper
1 cup (100g) coarsely grated
　mozzarella cheese

prep time: 25 minutes
(plus standing time)
cook time: 15 minutes
serves: 6
per serve: 14g fat; 84 cal

cauliflower au gratin

1 small (1kg) cauliflower
30g butter
1 tablespoon plain flour
2 spring onions, chopped
¾ cup (180ml) milk
¾ cup (90g) coarsely grated
    cheddar cheese
⅓ cup (35g) corn flakes,
    crushed into crumbs
15g butter, extra
1 tablespoon finely chopped
    fresh flat-leaf parsley

1 Trim cauliflower, cut into florets. Rinse florets under cold water; arrange in large shallow microwave-safe dish, stem ends towards edge of dish. Cook, covered, on HIGH (100%) 5 minutes; drain.

2 Melt butter in microwave-safe jug, uncovered, on HIGH (100%) 30 seconds. Whisk in flour and onion, then gradually whisk in milk; cook, uncovered, on HIGH (100%) about 2 minutes or until sauce boils and thickens, whisking once during cooking. Stir in cheese.

3 Combine crumbs, extra butter and parsley in small microwave-safe bowl; cook, uncovered, on HIGH (100%) 1 minute.

4 Pour sauce over cauliflower; cook, uncovered, on MEDIUM (55%) about 4 minutes or until hot. Sprinkle with crumb mixture.

prep time: 20 minutes
cook time: 15 minutes
serves: 6
per serve: 12.6g fat;
169 cal

broccoli with pine nuts

1 Cut broccoli into florets; rinse under cold water. Arrange florets in shallow microwave-safe dish, stem ends towards edge of dish. Cook, covered, on HIGH (100%) about 3 minutes or until just tender; drain.

2 Cook nuts on microwave-safe plate, uncovered, on HIGH (100%) about 3 minutes or until browned lightly, stirring twice during cooking.

3 Cook bacon between double thicknesses of absorbent paper, on HIGH (100%) about 3 minutes or until bacon is crisp.

4 Sprinkle nuts, bacon and cheeses over broccoli in dish; cook, uncovered, on MEDIUM (55%) about 2 minutes or until cheeses are melted.

800g broccoli
2 tablespoons pine nuts
3 bacon rashers, chopped finely
¼ cup (30g) coarsely grated cheddar cheese
¼ cup (20g) coarsely grated parmesan cheese

- prep time: 20 minutes
- cook time: 15 minutes
- serves: 6
- per serve: 10.6g fat; 150 cal

pak choy with mushrooms

400g pak choy
150g oyster mushrooms
½ teaspoon sesame oil
1 tablespoon salt-reduced
  soy sauce
1 tablespoon oyster sauce
1 tablespoon sesame seeds

1 Rinse pak choy well under cold water. Coarsely shred leaves; cut trimmed stems in half lengthways.

2 Place stems around edge of large shallow microwave-safe dish; place leaves in centre of dish. Cook, covered, on HIGH (100%) 2 minutes.

3 Combine mushrooms, oil, sauces and seeds in large microwave-safe bowl; cook, covered, on HIGH (100%) about 3 minutes or until mushrooms are tender, stirring once during cooking.

4 Combine drained bok choy and mushrooms in serving dish and mix well.

prep time: 10 minutes
cook time: 5 minutes
serves: 4
per serve: 2.3g fat; 48 cal

fresh asparagus with hollandaise sauce

1 Snap tough ends from asparagus. Arrange asparagus, thick ends towards edge of dish, in no more than 2 layers, in large microwave-safe dish, sprinkle with the water. Cook, covered, on HIGH (100%) 3 minutes; drain. Cover to keep warm.

2 Melt butter in microwave-safe jug, uncovered, on HIGH (100%) 1 minute. Whisk egg yolks, the extra water and juice in small microwave-safe bowl; cook, uncovered, on MEDIUM (55%) 1 minute, whisking every 15 seconds, or until sauce thickens. Do not allow to boil.

3 Remove sauce from microwave oven. Whisking constantly, add melted butter, a few drops at a time, until mixture starts to thicken. Continue to add butter, in a thin stream, whisking constantly, until all butter is used; whisk in pepper. Serve hollandaise sauce over hot asparagus.

500g fresh asparagus
1 tablespoon water
125g butter
2 egg yolks
1½ tablespoons water, extra
1 tablespoon lemon juice
pinch cayenne pepper

- prep time: 15 minutes
- cook time: 5 minutes
- serves: 4
- per serve: 128.5g fat; 275 cal

spicy vegetable dhal

1 cup (200g) red lentils

1 teaspoon chopped fresh
ginger

1 clove garlic, quartered

1 small fresh red chilli,
deseeded, chopped
coarsely

1 trimmed (75g) stick celery,
chopped finely

3 spring onions, chopped
coarsely

1 medium (120g) carrot,
chopped coarsely

2 tablespoons chopped
fresh coriander leaves

1 tablespoon lemon juice

3 cups (750ml) hot water

1 teaspoon garam masala

¼ teaspoon ground turmeric

1 teaspoon ground
coriander

1 teaspoon cumin seeds

1 Rinse and drain lentils. Combine lentils, ginger, garlic, chilli, celery, onion, carrot, fresh coriander, juice and the water in large microwave-safe bowl; cook, covered, on HIGH (100%) about 20 minutes or until lentils and vegetables are soft, stirring once during cooking. Cool.

2 Blend or process mixture, in batches, until smooth; return **to** same bowl.

3 Cook ground spices and seeds in small microwave-safe bowl, uncovered, on HIGH (100%) 1 minute; stir into lentil mixture. Cook, uncovered, on HIGH (100%) about 5 minutes or until dhal thickens, stirring once during cooking.

- prep time: 30 minutes
- cook time: 30 minutes
- serves: 6
- per serve: 0.7g fat; 97 cal
- tip: red lentils are called masoor dhal in Indian kitchens.

easy fried rice

1 Cook rice, rind and the water in large microwave-safe bowl, uncovered, on HIGH (100%) about 12 minutes or until rice is tender, stirring once during cooking. Rinse rice well; drain, discard rind.

2 Combine oil, bacon, carrot, celery, garlic and ginger in large microwave-safe bowl; cook, covered, on HIGH (100%) about 5 minutes or until vegetables are just tender, stirring once during cooking. Drain away excess liquid.

3 Add rice, mushrooms, onion and sauce to bowl; mix to combine. Cook, covered, on HIGH (100%) about 4 minutes or until hot.

1 cup (200g) white long-grain rice
6cm strip lemon rind
3 cups (750ml) boiling water
2 teaspoons vegetable oil
2 bacon rashers, chopped finely
1 medium (120g) carrot, sliced thinly
1 trimmed (75g) stick celery, sliced thinly
1 clove garlic, crushed
1 teaspoon grated fresh ginger
80g button mushrooms, sliced
2 spring onions, sliced
1 tablespoon soy sauce

- **prep time: 15 minutes**
- **cook time: 20 minutes**
- **serves: 4**
- **per serve: 6.3g fat; 260 cal**

curried vegetable & rice medley

1 small (150g) red pepper
2 medium (240g) carrots
2 teaspoons vegetable oil
1 medium (150g) brown onion, chopped finely
1 clove garlic, crushed
1 teaspoon mild curry powder
1 teaspoon ground cumin
2 tablespoons fruit chutney
250g broccoli, chopped
125g button mushrooms, sliced thinly
½ cup (125ml) vegetable stock
2 cups cooked white long-grain rice

1   Cut pepper and carrots into thin strips.
2   Combine oil, onion, garlic and spices in large microwave-safe bowl; cook, uncovered, on HIGH (100%) 4 minutes, stirring once during cooking.
3   Add chutney and vegetables; cook, covered, on HIGH (100%) 5 minutes.
4   Add stock and rice; cook, covered, on HIGH (100%) about 4 minutes or until hot, stirring once during cooking.

- prep time: 25 minutes
- cook time: 15 minutes
- serves: 6
- per serve: 2.1g fat; 101 cal
- tip: you will need to cook 2/3 cup (130g) white long-grain rice for this recipe.

spinach rice

1 Combine butter, oil, onion and garlic in large microwave-safe bowl; cook, uncovered, on HIGH (100%) 5 minutes, stirring once during cooking.

2 Add rice; cook, uncovered, on HIGH (100%) 1 minute.

3 Add stock; cook, covered, on HIGH (100%) 12 minutes, stirring once during cooking. Stand, covered, 5 minutes.

4 Add spinach, tomato and cheese; stir until spinach just wilts.

30g butter

1 tablespoon olive oil

2 medium (300g) brown onions, chopped finely

2 cloves garlic, crushed

2 cups (400g) white long-grain rice

1 litre (4 cups) boiling chicken stock

50g spinach, chopped

2 small (260g) tomatoes, deseeded, chopped

¼ cup (20g) finely grated parmesan cheese

- prep time: 20 minutes
- cook time: 25 minutes
- serves: 6
- per serve: 9.2g fat; 372 cal

baba ghanoush

2 large (1kg) aubergines
¼ cup (60ml) olive oil
2 tablespoons lemon juice
1 clove garlic, quartered
¼ cup (60ml) tahini
2 teaspoons ground cumin
⅔ cup fresh flat-leaf parsley
sprigs

1 Prick aubergines all over with fork; place on microwave turntable. Cook, uncovered, on HIGH (100%) about 15 minutes or until soft, rotating aubergines halfway through cooking. Stand aubergines 15 minutes.

2 Peel aubergines, chop flesh roughly.

3 Blend or process aubergine flesh with remaining ingredients until pureed.

prep time: 15 minutes
cook time: 30 minutes
serves: 4
per serve: 24.3g fat;
270 cal

caponata

1 Chop aubergines into 2cm cubes, place in colander, sprinkle with salt; stand 30 minutes. Rinse under cold water; drain on absorbent paper.

2 Combine oil and aubergine in large microwave-safe bowl; cook, uncovered, on HIGH (100%) about 10 minutes or until tender, stirring once during cooking. Remove from bowl.

3 Place onion, garlic and celery in same bowl; cook, covered, on HIGH (100%) about 10 minutes or until onion is very soft, stirring once during cooking.

4 Add olives, undrained crushed tomatoes and pepper; cook, uncovered, on HIGH (100%) 10 minutes, stirring once during cooking.

5 Stir in sugar, vinegar and capers; cook, uncovered, on HIGH (100%) 5 minutes. Stir in aubergine and herbs, cool.

2 small (460g) aubergines
coarse cooking salt
¼ cup (60ml) olive oil
4 medium (600g) brown onions, chopped
2 cloves garlic, crushed
2 trimmed (150g) sticks celery, chopped
1 cup (120g) pitted green olives, halved
2 x 400g cans tomatoes
1 teaspoon cracked black pepper
1 tablespoon sugar
½ cup (125ml) red wine vinegar
2 tablespoons drained capers
2 tablespoons chopped fresh flat-leaf parsley
2 tablespoons chopped fresh basil leaves

- prep time: 25 minutes (plus standing Time)
- cook time: 35 minutes
- serves: 6
- per serve: 10.9g fat; 181 cal

Cooking vegetables

The microwave oven is ideal for cooking vegetables as they retain their colour, flavour and nutrients – and take only minutes to cook! Here's a quick guide on cooking a variety of fresh vegies.

artichokes
quantity: 5 medium (1kg) globe
to cook: Trim bases to sit flat, discard tough outer leaves, rinse well. Place artichokes and 60ml water in large microwave-safe dish; cover. Microwave on HIGH (100%) 15 minutes, turning halfway during cooking. Drain upside down; remove hairy choke with a spoon, discard.

asparagus
quantity: 500g
to cook: Snap off woody ends, peel lower part of stem with vegetable peeler if stems are thick. Place asparagus and 2 tablespoons water in large microwave-safe dish; cover. Microwave on HIGH (100%) about 3 minutes or until tender. Drain.

beans, green
quantity: 500g
to cook: Trim beans as desired. Place green beans and 2 tablespoons water in large microwave-safe dish; cover. Microwave on HIGH (100%) about 4 minutes or until tender, stirring halfway. Stand 1 minute before serving. Drain.

beans, butter
quantity: 500g
to cook: Trim and place beans and 2 tablespoons water in large microwave-safe dish; cover. Microwave on HIGH (100%) about 4 minutes or until tender, stirring halfway. Stand 1 minute before serving. Drain.

beans, broad
quantity: 1kg
to cook: Shell and place beans and 60ml water in large microwave-safe bowl; cover. Microwave on HIGH (100%) about 6 minutes or until tender, stirring halfway during cooking. Drain then refresh under cold water; drain again.

beetroot
quantity: 3 medium (500g), unpeeled, with 3cm of stem remaining
to cook: Place beetroot and 2 tablespoons water in large microwave-safe dish; cover. Microwave on HIGH (100%) about 30 minutes or until tender, stirring halfway during cooking. Drain, peel while still warm.

broccoflower
quantity: 500g
to cook: Cut into florets. Place florets and 60ml water in large microwave-safe dish; cover. Microwave on HIGH (100%) about 3 minutes or until tender, stirring halfway during cooking time. Drain.

broccoli
quantity: 500g
to cook: Cut into florets. Place florets and 60ml water in medium microwave-safe dish; cover. Microwave on HIGH (100%) about 5 minutes or until tender, stirring halfway during cooking time. Drain.

brussels sprouts
quantity: 1kg
to cook: Cut a cross in base of each sprout; place sprouts and 60ml water in large microwave-safe dish; cover. Microwave on HIGH (100%) about 8 minutes or until tender, stirring halfway during cooking time. Drain.

cabbage
quantity: 900g
to cook: Chop coarsely and place with 2 tablespoons water in large microwave-safe dish; cover. Microwave on HIGH (100%) about 9 minutes or until tender, stirring halfway during cooking time. Drain.

carrots
quantity: 3 large (540g)
to cook: Peel and cut into 1cm slices. Place carrots and 60ml water in large microwave-safe dish; cover. Microwave on HIGH (100%) about 8 minutes or until tender, stirring halfway during cooking time. Drain.

cauliflower
quantity: 500g
to cook: Cut into florets. Place cauliflower and 60ml water in large microwave-safe dish; cover. Microwave on HIGH (100%) about 6 minutes or until tender, stirring halfway during cooking. Stand 1 minute. Drain.

celeriac
quantity: 1 large (1.25kg)
to cook: Peel and cut into 2cm pieces. Place celeriac and 60ml water in large microwave-safe dish; cover. Microwave on HIGH (100%) about 20 minutes or until tender, stirring halfway during cooking. Stand 2 minutes. Drain.

corn on the cob
quantity: 2 medium (600g)
to cook: Remove and discard husk and silk. Place corn and 1 tablespoon water in medium microwave-safe dish; cover. Microwave on HIGH (100%) about 5 minutes or until tender, turning halfway during cooking time. Drain.

courgettes
quantity: 4 medium (500g)
to cook: Trim and halve crossways. Place courgettes and 2 tablespoons water in medium microwave-safe dish; cover. Microwave on HIGH (100%) about 5 minutes or until tender, stirring halfway during cooking time. Drain.

fennel
quantity: 2 medium (1.2kg)
to cook: Remove stalks and leaves from fennel bulbs, halve

lengthways, trim bases to separate halves. Place fennel and 60ml water in large microwave-safe bowl; cover. Microwave on HIGH (100%) 5 minutes or until tender, stirring halfway. Drain.

gai lan (Chinese broccoli)
quantity: 900g
to cook: Trim and chop. Place gai lan with 1 tablespoon water in large microwave-safe dish; cover. Microwave on HIGH (100%) about 3 minutes or until tender, stirring halfway during cooking time. Drain.

kohlrabi
quantity: 3 medium (1.5kg)
to cook: Remove leaves, peel and chop into 3cm pieces. Place kohlrabi and 2 tablespoons water in large microwave-safe bowl; cover. Microwave on HIGH (100%: about 12 minutes or until tender, stirring halfway during cooking time. Drain.

mangetout
quantity: 250g
to cook: Trim ends. Place mangetout and 2 teaspoons water in large microwave-safe dish; cover. Microwave on HIGH (100%) about 2 minutes or until tender, stirring halfway during cooking time. Drain.

pak choy
quantity: 800g
to cook: Trim bases; separate leaves. Place pak choy and 1 tablespoon water in large microwave-safe dish; cover. Microwave on HIGH (100%) about 3 minutes or until tender, stirring halfway during cooking time. Drain.

parsnips
quantity: 4 medium (500g)
to cook: Peel and chop coarsely. Place parsnips and 2 tablespoons

water in large microwave-safe dish; cover. Microwave time on HIGH (100%) about 6 minutes or until tender, turning halfway during cooking time. Drain.

pattypan squash
quantity: 500g
to cook: Trim and quarter. Place squash and 2 tablespoons water in medium microwave-safe dish; cover. Microwave on HIGH (100%) about 4 minutes or until tender, stirring halfway during cooking time. Drain.

peas, green
quantity: 500g
to cook: Shell and place peas and 1 tablespoon water in large microwave-safe dish; cover. Microwave on HIGH (100%) about 3 minutes or until tender, stirring halfway during cooking time. Drain.

peas, sugar snap
quantity: 250g
to cook: Trim ends, remove strings. Place peas and 2 teaspoons water in large microwave-safe dish; cover. Microwave on HIGH (100%) about 2 minutes or until tender, stirring halfway during cooking time. Drain.

potatoes
quantity: 5 medium (1kg)
to cook: Peel and quarter. Place potatoes and 2 tablespoons water in large microwave-safe dish; cover. Microwave on HIGH (100%) about 10 minutes or until just tender, stirring halfway during cooking time. Drain.

pumpkin/butternut squash
quantity: 500g
to cook: Peel, deseed and chop. Place pumpkin and 1 tablespoon water in large microwave-safe dish; cover. Microwave on HIGH (100%) about 5 minutes or until tender, stirring halfway during cooking time. Drain.

spinach
quantity: 350g
to cook: Cut off and discard roots and about 6cm of lower stems, wash leaves thoroughly. Place spinach in large microwave-safe bowl; cover. Microwave time on HIGH (100%): about 2 minutes or until just wilted; refresh under cold water. Drain well.

swedes
quantity: 4 medium (500g)
to cook: Peel thickly and chop into 3cm pieces. Place in large microwave-safe dish; cover. Microwave on HIGH (100%) about 8 minutes or until tender, stirring halfway during cooking time. Drain.

sweet potatoes
quantity: 2 large (1kg)
to cook: Peel and slice into 2cm rounds. Place sweet potatoes and 2 tablespoons water in large microwave-safe dish; cover. Microwave on HIGH (100%) about 10 minutes or until tender, stirring halfway during cooking time. Drain.

swiss chard
quantity: 500g
to cook: Cut off and discard white stems, wash leaves thoroughly. Place whole leaves in large microwave-safe dish; cover. Microwave on HIGH (100%) about 4 minutes or until tender, stirring halfway during cooking time. Drain well.

tat soi
quantity: 300g tat soi
to cook: Trim bases, separate leaves. Place tat soi and 1 tablespoon water in large microwave-safe dish; cover. Microwave on HIGH (100%) about 3 minutes or until tender, stirring halfway during cooking time. Drain.

turnips
quantity: 4 medium (500g)
to cook: Thickly peel and coarsely chop. Place turnips and 1 tablespoon water in large microwave-safe dish; cover. Microwave on HIGH (100%) about 6 minutes or until tender, stirring halfway during cooking time. Drain.

Sweet treats

poached peaches & custard

3 cups (750ml) water
1 cup (250ml) orange juice
1½ cups (330g) caster sugar
4 medium (800g) firm
  peaches
1 teaspoon cornflour
2 teaspoons water, extra
custard
1 cup (250ml) milk
3 egg yolks
⅓ cup (75g) caster sugar

1 Combine the water, juice and sugar in large microwave-safe bowl; cook, uncovered, on HIGH (100%) about 3 minutes or until sugar dissolves, stirring twice during cooking.
2 Add peaches; cook, covered, on HIGH (100%) about 6 minutes or until tender. Cover peaches; refrigerate 3 hours.
3 Remove peaches from syrup; peel, reserve syrup.
4 Strain 1 cup (250ml) syrup into microwave-safe jug; stir in blended cornflour and extra water. Cook, uncovered, on HIGH (100%) about 3 minutes or until syrup boils and thickens slightly, whisking twice during cooking; cool.
5 Serve peaches with syrup and custard.
custard Heat milk in microwave-safe jug on MEDIUM-HIGH (70%) 1 minute. Whisk in combined egg yolks and sugar; cook, uncovered, on MEDIUM (55%) about 5 minutes or until custard thickens slightly, whisking twice during cooking. Cover surface closely with cling film; refrigerate until required.

- **prep time: 20 minutes**
  (plus refrigeration)
- **cook time: 20 minutes**
- **serves: 4**
- **per serve: 6.8g fat; 549 cal**

Cook's tip

To melt chocolate, place 100g chopped chocolate in a small microwave-safe bowl; cook, uncovered, on MEDIUM (55%) about 2 minutes. Chocolate will hold its shape after heating; stir before cooking further.

poached pears
with cinnamon cream

4 small (720g) firm pears
1 cup (250ml) dry red wine
1 cup (250ml) water
½ cup (110g) caster sugar
1 cinnamon stick
1 tablespoon caster sugar,
    extra
1 teaspoon cornflour
2 teaspoons water, extra
cinnamon cream
300ml whipping cream
1 tablespoon caster sugar
1 teaspoon ground
    cinnamon

1 Level bases of pears to sit flat; peel. Combine wine, the water, sugar and cinnamon stick in large microwave-safe dish; cook, uncovered, on HIGH (100%) 3 minutes. Stir until sugar dissolves.

2 Place pears upright in poaching syrup; cook, covered, on HIGH (100%) 5 minutes. Rotate pears 180 degrees; cook, covered, on HIGH (100%) about 5 minutes or until just tender. Refrigerate pears several hours, turning pears occasionally to coat with syrup.

3 Remove pears from syrup; strain ¾ cup (180ml) syrup into small microwave-safe bowl. Stir in extra sugar and cornflour blended with extra water; cook, uncovered, on HIGH (100%) about 3 minutes or until sauce boils and thickens, whisking once during cooking. Cool. Serve pears with syrup and cinnamon cream.

cinnamon cream Beat all ingredients in small bowl with electric mixer until soft peaks form.

- prep time: 20 minutes
  (plus refrigeration time)
- cook time: 20 minutes
- serves: 4
- per serve: 27.8g fat;
  519 cal

strawberry-glazed cheesecakes

1 Grease four 310ml microwave-safe dishes, line bases of each dish with baking parchment.

2 Combine biscuit crumbs and butter in small bowl; divide among prepared dishes, press over bases. Pour filling into prepared dishes; refrigerate about 3 hours or until set.

3 Just before serving, run a knife around edge of dishes. Turn out cheesecakes; brush tops with sieved jam, decorate with strawberries, brush with remaining jam.

filling Beat softened cream cheese, sugar and cornflour in small bowl with electric mixer until combined. Add remaining ingredients; beat until smooth. Transfer mixture to large microwave-safe bowl; cook, uncovered, on MEDIUM (55%) about 10 minutes or until mixture is extremely thick, whisking after each minute.

1½ cups (150g) digestive
  biscuit crumbs
80g butter, melted
¼ cup (60ml) strawberry jam,
  warmed
250g strawberries, halved
filling
250g cream cheese
⅓ cup (75g) caster sugar
2 tablespoons cornflour
300ml soured cream
3 eggs, beaten lightly
2 teaspoons finely grated
  lemon rind
2 teaspoons lemon juice

- prep time: 30 minutes
  (plus refrigeration time)
- cook time: 30 minutes
- serves: 4
- per serve: 77.7g fat;
  1012 cal

lemon delicious

2 egg yolks
½ cup (110g) caster sugar
2 teaspoons grated lemon
   rind
⅓ cup (50g) self-raising flour
1 teaspoon ground ginger
¼ cup (60ml) lemon juice
¾ cup (180ml) milk
40g butter, melted
3 egg whites

1 Grease deep 1-litre microwave-safe dish.
2 Beat egg yolks, sugar and rind in small bowl with electric mixer until thick and creamy. Gently fold in flour and ginger, then juice, milk and butter.
3 Beat egg whites in small bowl with electric mixer until soft peaks form; fold into lemon mixture in 2 batches.
4 Spoon into prepared dish; cook, uncovered, on MEDIUM-HIGH (70%) about 5 minutes or until centre is almost set. Stand 5 minutes. Dust with sifted icing sugar, if desired.

prep time: 20 minutes
cook time: 10 minutes
serves: 4
per serve: 13.5g fat;
302 cal

apple & pear crumble

1 Place apple, pear, sugar and honey in shallow 2-litre microwave-safe dish; cook, covered, on HIGH (100%) about 5 minutes or until fruit is just tender, stirring once during cooking.

2 Sprinkle with crumble topping; cook, uncovered, on HIGH (100%) about 6 minutes or until topping is firm.

crumble topping Combine flour, cinnamon, oats and coconut in bowl; rub in butter, stir in sugar.

3 large (600g) apples, peeled, cored, sliced
3 small (540g) pears, peeled, cored, sliced
1 tablespoon caster sugar
1 tablespoon honey
crumble topping
½ cup (75g) self-raising flour
1 teaspoon ground cinnamon
¾ cup (65g) rolled oats
⅓ cup (30g) desiccated coconut
75g cold butter
⅓ cup (75g) firmly packed brown sugar

- prep time: 25 minutes
- cook time: 12 minutes
- serves: 4
- per serve: 22.2g fat; 528 cal

lemon & blueberry self-saucing pudding

60g butter

1½ cups (225g) self-raising flour

1 cup (220g) caster sugar

1 tablespoon grated lemon rind

¾ cup (180ml) milk

1 cup (150g) fresh blueberries

1 cup (200g) firmly packed brown sugar

½ cup (125ml) lemon juice

1½ cups (375ml) boiling water

1 Melt butter in a deep 3-litre microwave-safe dish, uncovered, on HIGH (100%) 1 minute.

2 Add flour, caster sugar, rind and milk; whisk until smooth, stir in blueberries.

3 Sprinkle brown sugar evenly over top; carefully pour combined juice and boiling water over brown sugar.

4 Cook, uncovered, on HIGH (100%) about 12 minutes or until just cooked in centre; stand 5 minutes before serving.

- prep time: 15 minutes
- cook time: 20 minutes
- serves: 6
- per serve: 9.9g fat; 501 cal

mocha self-saucing pudding

1 Melt butter in deep 3-litre microwave-safe dish, uncovered, on HIGH (100%) 1 minute. Stir in caster sugar, flour, milk and half the cocoa; whisk until smooth.

2 Sift combined remaining cocoa, brown sugar and coffee powder evenly over top; carefully pour the boiling water over brown sugar mixture.

3 Cook, uncovered, on HIGH (100%) about 12 minutes or until just cooked in centre; stand 5 minutes before serving.

60g butter
1 cup (220g) caster sugar
1½ cups (225g) self-raising flour
¾ cup (180ml) milk
½ cup (50g) cocoa
1 cup (200g) firmly packed brown sugar
2 teaspoons instant coffee powder
2 cups (500ml) boiling water

- **prep time: 15 minutes**
- **cook time: 20 minutes**
- **serves: 6**
- **per serve: 11g fat; 508 cal**

sticky toffee pudding

1 cup (170g) pitted dates,
  chopped
1¼ cups (310ml) hot water
1 teaspoon bicarbonate of
  soda
80g butter, chopped
¾ cup (165g) raw sugar
2 eggs
1¼ cups (185g) self-raising
  flour

caramel sauce
¾ cup (150g) firmly packed
  brown sugar
⅔ cup (160ml) double cream
30g butter, chopped

1 Lightly grease 21cm microwave-safe ring cake pan, line base with baking parchment.
2 Combine dates and water in medium microwave-safe bowl; cook, uncovered on HIGH (100%) 4 minutes, stirring once during cooking.
3 Stir in bicarbonate of soda (mixture will foam); let cool 5 minutes.
4 Blend or process date mixture with remaining ingredients until combined; spread into prepared pan.
5 Cook, uncovered, on MEDIUM-HIGH (70%) 8 minutes. Stand 5 minutes before turning onto wire rack to cool. Serve warm with caramel sauce.

caramel sauce Combine all ingredients in medium microwave-safe bowl. Cook, uncovered, on HIGH (100%) about 7 minutes or until caramel has thickened, whisking after each minute.

- prep time: 25 minutes
- cook time: 25 minutes
- serves: 8
- per serve: 21.8g fat;
  485 cal

Cook's tip

This mixture will also make 18 sticky toffee pudding muffins. Pour mixture into 18 holes of lightly greased 80ml capacity microwave-safe muffin pans. Cook each pan, uncovered, on MEDIUM-HIGH (70%) about 3½ minutes or until muffins are almost cooked through.

easy christmas pudding

2¾ cups (500g) mixed dried fruit

⅓ cup (80ml) brandy or orange juice

125g butter, softened

¾ cup (150g) firmly packed brown sugar

2 tablespoons golden syrup

2 eggs

1 teaspoon Parisian essence (see tip)

1 large (200g) apple, peeled, cored, grated

¾ cup (110g) plain flour

2 teaspoons mixed spice

½ teaspoon bicarbonate of soda

1 Grease 2.5-litre microwave-safe bowl, line base with baking parchment.

2 Combine fruit and brandy in another large microwave-safe bowl; cook, covered, on HIGH (100%) 1 minute, cool slightly.

3 Beat butter, sugar and syrup in small bowl with electric mixer until just combined. Beat in eggs, 1 at a time. Add to fruit mixture with essence, apple and sifted dry ingredients. Spoon mixture into prepared bowl; smooth top.

4 Cook, uncovered, on MEDIUM (55%) 10 minutes. Rotate bowl 180 degrees; cook, uncovered, on MEDIUM (55%) about 10 minutes or until centre of pudding is almost cooked. Stand, covered, 15 minutes before turning onto serving plate.

- prep time: 20 minutes
- cook time: 35 minutes
- serves: 8
- per serve: 15.3g fat; 470 cal
- tip: Parisian essence is a flavourless liquid used to give food a brown colour, but it is not essential in making this pudding.

apple & pecan cake

1 Grease 21cm microwave-safe ring cake pan, sprinkle base and sides with ground hazelnuts.

2 Beat butter, flour, cinnamon, sugar, syrup and eggs in medium bowl with electric mixer, on low speed, until ingredients are combined. Then beat on medium speed about 2 minutes or until mixture is smooth and changed in colour.

3 Stir in nuts, raisins and apple. Spread mixture into prepared pan; cook, uncovered, on MEDIUM-HIGH (70%) about 10 minutes or until just cooked. Stand 5 minutes before turning onto wire rack to cool.

⅓ cup (35g) ground hazelnuts

90g butter, softened

1½ cups (225g) self-raising flour

1 teaspoon ground cinnamon

¾ cup (150g) firmly packed brown sugar

¼ cup (60ml) maple-flavoured syrup

3 eggs

1 cup (125g) chopped pecans

½ cup (85g) chopped raisins

1 large (200g) apple, peeled, grated

- prep time: 20 minutes
- cook time: 15 minutes
- serves: 8
- per serve: 26g fat; 479 cal

moist carrot cake

1 cup (150g) self-raising flour
¾ cup (150g) firmly packed
    brown sugar
2 teaspoons ground
    cinnamon
2 cups coarsely grated carrot
½ cup (85g) chopped raisins
½ cup (125ml) vegetable oil
2 eggs
⅓ cup (40g) chopped
    walnuts
cream cheese frosting
60g cream cheese
30g butter
1½ cups (240g) icing sugar
2 teaspoons lemon juice

1 Grease 21cm microwave-safe ring cake pan, line base with baking parchment.

2 Combine flour, sugar, cinnamon, carrot and raisins in large bowl; stir in oil and eggs.

3 Pour mixture into prepared pan; cook, uncovered, on MEDIUM-HIGH (70%) about 10 minutes or until just cooked. Stand cake 5 minutes before turning onto wire rack to cool. Top with frosting and walnuts.

cream cheese frosting Beat cream cheese and butter in small bowl with electric mixer until smooth; gradually add icing sugar and juice, beat until combined.

- prep time: 25 minutes
  (plus cooling time)
- cook time: 15 minutes
- serves: 8
- per serve: 26g fat; 533 cal
- tip: You will need about
  4 medium (480g) carrots
  for this recipe.

one-bowl chocolate cake

1 Grease 21cm microwave-safe ring cake pan, line with baking parchment.

2 Combine butter, sugar and the water in large microwave-safe bowl; cook, uncovered, on HIGH (100%) 4 minutes, stirring once during cooking. Cool to room temperature.

3 Sift dry ingredients into butter mixture; whisk mixture until smooth, stir in egg.

4 Pour mixture into prepared pan; cook, uncovered, on MEDIUM-HIGH (70%) about 10 minutes or until just cooked. Stand 5 minutes before turning onto wire rack to cool.

5 Spread with fudge frosting.

fudge frosting Combine butter, the water and caster sugar in small microwave-safe bowl; cook, uncovered, on HIGH (100%) 1 minute, stir until sugar dissolves. Whisk in sifted icing sugar and cocoa. Cover; refrigerate 30 minutes or until frosting thickens. Beat until a spreadable consistency.

125g butter
1 cup (220g) caster sugar
1 cup (250ml) water
1½ cups (225g) self-raising flour
⅓ cup (35g) cocoa
½ teaspoon bicarbonate of soda
2 eggs, beaten lightly
fudge frosting
45g butter
2 tablespoons water
¼ cup (55g) caster sugar
¾ cup (120g) icing sugar
2 tablespoons cocoa

prep time: 20 minutes (plus refrigeration time)
cook time: 20 minutes
serves: 4
per serve: 20.3g fat; 479 cal

courgette walnut loaf

⅓ cup (40g) walnut pieces
2 eggs
¾ cup (150g) firmly packed
  brown sugar
¾ cup (180ml) vegetable oil
1 teaspoon mixed spice
1 cup coarsely grated
  courgettes
⅔ cup (80g) walnut pieces,
  extra
¾ cup (110g) plain flour
1 cup (150g) self-raising flour

1 Grease 12cm x 22cm microwave-safe loaf pan; line base with baking parchment. Crush nuts finely, press half onto sides of pan.

2 Whisk eggs, sugar, oil and spice in large bowl until smooth; add, in 2 batches, courgette, extra nuts and flours. Spread mixture into prepared pan; sprinkle with remaining crushed walnuts.

3 Cook, uncovered, on MEDIUM-HIGH (70%) about 9 minutes or until centre is just cooked.

4 Cover with greased foil; stand 10 minutes before turning onto wire rack to cool.

- prep time: 20 minutes
- cook time: 20 minutes
- serves: 8
- per serve: 33.9g fat;
  495 cal
- tip: You will need about
  2 small (180g) courgettes
  for this recipe.

pumpkin pecan muffins

1 Grease two 6-hole (80ml) microwave-safe muffin pans.

2 Combine flour, spices, sugar, oil, egg, pumpkin, nuts and cream in large bowl, stir until just combined. Spoon mixture into prepared pans; sprinkle with extra nuts.

3 Cook 1 pan at a time, uncovered, on MEDIUM-HIGH (70%) about 4 minutes or until muffins are just cooked in the centre. Stand 1 minute before turning muffins onto wire rack.

1½ cups (225g) self-raising flour
½ teaspoon ground cinnamon
½ teaspoon mixed spice
⅓ cup (75g) firmly packed brown sugar
⅓ cup (80ml) vegetable oil
2 eggs, beaten lightly
¾ cup cooked mashed pumpkin or butternut squash
½ cup (60g) chopped pecans
¼ cup (60ml) double cream
¼ cup (30g) chopped pecans, extra

- prep time: 20 minutes
- cook time: 10 minutes
- makes: 12
- per muffin: 15.3g fat; 239 cal
- tip: You will need to cook about 300g pumpkin or butternut squash for this recipe.

peanut cookies

½ cup (130g) smooth peanut butter
90g soft butter
¾ cup (165g) raw sugar
1 egg
1 teaspoon vanilla essence
1½ cups (225g) plain flour
½ cup (75g) unsalted roasted peanuts
14 red glacé cherries, halved

1 Beat peanut butter, butter, sugar, egg, essence and flour in small bowl with electric mixer until combined; stir in peanuts.
2 Roll level tablespoons of mixture into balls. Cover microwave turntable with baking parchment, place 7 balls evenly around turntable about 2cm from edge.
3 Flatten balls slightly, top with cherry halves. Cook, uncovered, on HIGH (100%) 2 minutes.
4 Slide paper and cookies onto wire rack; stand 5 minutes before lifting from paper onto rack to cool. Repeat with remaining mixture and cherries.

- prep time: 20 minutes
- cook time: 8 minutes
- makes: 28
- per cookie: 6.6g fat; 126 cal

chocolate caramel slice

1 Grease shallow 18cm x 28cm microwave-safe dish, line base and sides with baking parchment.

2 Cook coconut in medium microwave-safe bowl, uncovered, on HIGH (100%) about 3 minutes or until browned lightly, stirring 3 times during cooking; remove from bowl, cool.

3 Melt butter in same bowl, uncovered, on HIGH (100%) 1 minute. Add coconut and crumbs, stir well. Press over base of prepared dish, refrigerate until firm.

4 Combine milk, extra butter and syrup in large glass microwave-safe bowl; cook, uncovered, on HIGH (100%) about 8 minutes until thick and golden brown, whisking every minute. Spread quickly over biscuit base; refrigerate until firm.

5 Melt chocolate with oil in small microwave-safe bowl, uncovered, on MEDIUM (55%) 1½ minutes, stirring twice during cooking. Spread over caramel mixture. Mark chocolate with fork; refrigerate slice until firm.

½ cup (45g) desiccated coconut

160g butter, melted

2 cups (200g) plain chocolate biscuit crumbs

400g can sweetened condensed milk

60g butter, extra

2 tablespoons maple-flavoured syrup

100g dark chocolate, chopped

2 teaspoons vegetable oil

- prep time: 20 minutes (plus refrigeration Time)
- cook time: 15 minutes
- makes: 27 pieces
- per piece: 11.9g fat; 179 cal

Preserves

tips for making preserves

- As a guide, do not use more than 500g of fruit and vegetables for each recipe, as small quantities work best in the microwave oven.

- Since there is a minimal amount of evaporation of liquid during cooking in the microwave oven, there is generally less liquid used in recipes than in conventional recipes.

- Always use a large shallow microwave-safe dish for cooking preserves, and check the preserve often during cooking time; stir gently to check consistency.

- Cover preserves during cooking only when specified.

- After the minimum suggested cooking time, open the oven door and allow bubbles to subside. Drop a teaspoon of the preserve onto a cold plate; cool to room temperature. If the cooled preserve is the consistency you're after, it is ready to bottle. If not, continue to cook.

- Cooking times given in recipes are a guide only; times vary depending on the type of oven and utensils used, as well as on the ripeness and water content of the fruit and vegetables.

- All fruit – especially citrus rinds – must be softened before adding sugar. Sugar must be dissolved before the mixture boils.

- Butters, spreads and curds based on butter and/or eggs require careful monitoring during cooking; they will curdle and separate if they are allowed to boil.

- All preserves must be poured, while hot, into hot sterilised jars or bottles; seal immediately.

- Follow individual recipes for storage times. Always store opened jars or bottles, covered, in the refrigerator. Unopened jars or bottles can be stored in the pantry but, if you live in a humid climate, the refrigerator is the best place to store preserves.

- Sterilise jars and bottles by placing them and their metal lids in a large pan filled with cold water; cover, turn heat to maximum. When water boils, remove pan lid; boil 20 minutes. Using oven mitts and kitchen tongs, remove jars and lids from pan; drain excess water from jars, stand upright to allow any remaining water to evaporate. You can also wash jars in your dishwasher without detergent. It is important to use jars while they are hot and to seal them while still hot.

peach & passionfruit jam

1 medium (180g) orange
1 medium (140g) lemon
2 tablespoons water
1 cup (250ml) water, extra
5 medium (1kg) peaches,
  peeled, sliced thinly
4 cups (880g) caster sugar,
  approximately
⅔ cup (160ml) passionfruit
  pulp

1 Remove and reserve seeds from unpeeled roughly chopped orange and lemon. Put seeds and the 2 tablespoons water in small bowl; cover, stand mixture overnight.

2 Blend or process orange and lemon until finely chopped. Combine fruit mixture with the 1 cup extra water in large glass microwave-safe bowl, cover; stand overnight.

3 Next day, drain seeds over fruit mixture; discard seeds.

4 Cook, covered, on HIGH (100%) 15 minutes, stirring once during cooking. Add peaches; cook, uncovered, on HIGH (100%) about 10 minutes or until peaches are soft and pulpy, stirring once during cooking.

5 Measure fruit mixture; allow 1 cup (220g) sugar for every 1 cup fruit mixture. Return fruit mixture and sugar to same bowl, stir until sugar dissolves.

6 Cook, uncovered, on HIGH (100%) about 25 minutes or until jam jells when tested, stirring 3 times during cooking. Skim surface; gently stir in passionfruit pulp; stand 5 minutes. Pour into hot sterilised jars; seal while hot.

- **prep time: 30 minutes**
  (plus standing time)
- **cook time: 1 hour**
- **makes: about 1.25 litres**
- **store: refrigerated for**
  2 months
- **per serve: 0g fat; 32 cal**
- **tip: You will need about**
  8 passionfruit for this
  recipe.

apricot citrus marmalade

1   Remove and reserve seeds from unpeeled quartered orange and lemon. Put seeds and the 1 tablespoon water in small bowl; cover, stand overnight.

2   Roughly chop orange, lemon and apricots; blend or process until finely chopped. Combine fruit with the 2 cups extra water in large glass microwave-safe bowl.

3   Cook, covered, on HIGH (100%) about 20 minutes or until rind is soft, stirring once during cooking. Do not uncover; stand fruit mixture overnight.

4   Next day, drain seeds over fruit mixture; discard seeds.

5   Measure fruit mixture; allow 1 cup (220g) sugar for every 1 cup fruit mixture. Return fruit mixture and sugar to same bowl; cook, uncovered, on HIGH (100%) 5 minutes, stirring twice during cooking.

6   Cook, uncovered, without stirring, on HIGH (100%) about 5 minutes or until marmalade jells when tested. Skim surface, pour into hot sterilised jars; seal while hot.

1 medium (180g) orange
1 large (180g) lemon
1 tablespoon water
¾ cup (110g) dried apricots
2 cups (500ml) water, extra
2½ cups (550g) caster sugar, approximately

- prep time: 25 minutes (plus standing time)
- cook time: 30 minutes
- serves: about 875ml
- store: refrigerated for 2 months
- per serve: 0g fat; 29 cal

rhubarb berry jam

4 cups (440g) chopped
 rhubarb
500g fresh or frozen
 blackberries
1 teaspoon finely grated
 orange rind
1 tablespoon orange juice
1 tablespoon lemon juice
1¾ cups (385g) caster sugar

1 Combine rhubarb, berries, rind and juices in large glass microwave-safe bowl; cook, uncovered, on HIGH (100%) 10 minutes, stirring once during cooking.

2 Add sugar, stir until sugar dissolves. Cook, uncovered, on HIGH (100%) about 20 minutes or until jam jells when tested, stirring 3 times during cooking. Pour into hot sterilised jars; seal while hot.

Rhubarb Berry Jam

- prep time: 15 minutes
- cook time: 30 minutes
- makes: about 750ml
- store: refrigerated for
  2 months
- per serve: 0g fat; 24 cal

apricot & passionfruit jam

1 Combine apricots, juice and the water in large glass microwave-safe bowl; cook, uncovered, on HIGH (100%) 15 minutes, stirring once during cooking.

2 Add sugar, stir until sugar dissolves. Cook, uncovered, on HIGH (100%) about 10 minutes or until jam jells when tested, stirring 3 times during cooking.

3 Add passionfruit pulp; stand 2 minutes, stir jam to distribute seeds. Pour into hot sterilised jars; seal while hot.

500g dried apricots, halved
¼ cup (60ml) lemon juice
2 cups (500ml) water
4 cups (880g) caster sugar
½ cup (125ml) passionfruit
   pulp

- prep time: 15 minutes
- cook time: 25 minutes
- makes: about 1.25 litres
- store: refrigerated for
  2 months
- per serve: 0g fat; 37 cal
- tip: You will need about
  6 passionfruit for this
  recipe.

fruit salad jam

250g dried apricots
2 cups (500ml) water
1 cup (250ml) undrained
   crushed pineapple in syrup
½ cup (125ml) orange juice
¼ cup (60ml) passionfruit
   pulp
3 cups (660g) caster sugar
3 large (700g) bananas,
   sliced

1   Cook apricots and water in large glass microwave-safe bowl, uncovered, on HIGH (100%) 5 minutes, stand 10 minutes.
2   Stir in pineapple; cook, uncovered, on HIGH (100%) 15 minutes. Stir in juice and pulp; cook, uncovered, on HIGH (100%) 10 minutes.
3   Add sugar, stir until sugar dissolves.
4   Add banana; cook, uncovered, on HIGH (100%) about 20 minutes or until jam jells when tested, stirring 3 times during cooking. Stand 5 minutes; skim surface. Pour into hot sterilised jars; seal while hot.

- prep time: 15 minutes
- cook time: 50 minutes
- makes: about 1.25 litres
- store: refrigerated for
  2 months
- per serve: 0g fat; 32 cal
- tip: You will need
  3 passionfruit for this
  recipe.

citrus butter

1 Whisk eggs and sugar together in large glass microwave-safe bowl; gently stir in remaining ingredients.
2 Cook butter mixture, uncovered, on MEDIUM (55%) 6 minutes, whisking every 2 minutes.
3 Then cook mixture, uncovered, on MEDIUM (55%) for a further 2 minutes or until it thickens, whisking once during cooking. Pour into hot sterilised jars; seal while hot.

4 eggs
¾ cup (165g) sugar
1 teaspoon finely grated
 lemon rind
¼ cup (60ml) lemon juice
1 teaspoon finely grated
 orange rind
¼ cup (60ml) orange juice
¼ cup (60ml) water
125g unsalted butter,
 chopped

- prep time: 25 minutes
- cook time: 10 minutes
- makes: about 500ml
- storage: refrigerated for
  1 month
- per serve: 2.5g fat; 39 cal

tangy strawberry jam

500g strawberries, hulled,
  quartered
¼ cup (60ml) lemon juice
2 cups (440g) caster sugar
2 tablespoons Grand Marnier

- prep time: 15 minutes
- cook time: 20 minutes
- makes: about 375ml
- store: refrigerated for
  2 months
- per serve: 13.9g fat;
  54 cal
- tip: Grand Marnier is an
  orange-flavoured liqueur.
  You can substitute
  Cointreau or Triple Sec,
  if desired.

1 Cook strawberries and
juice in large glass
microwave-safe bowl,
uncovered, on HIGH (100%)
5 minutes. Add sugar, stir until
sugar dissolves.
2 Cook, uncovered, on HIGH
(100%) about 15 minutes or
until jam jells when tested,
stirring 3 times during
cooking. Stir in liqueur. Pour
into hot sterilised jars; seal
while hot.

tomato & apple jam

4 medium (750g) tomatoes,
  peeled
1 small (130g) apple, peeled,
  grated coarsely
75g finely chopped stem
  ginger
¼ cup (60ml) lemon juice
2 cups (440g) caster sugar

- prep time: 15 minutes
- cook time: 35 minutes
- makes: about 625ml
- store: refrigerated for
  2 months
- per serve: 0g fat; 35 cal

1 Roughly chop tomatoes,
combine with apple and
ginger in large glass
microwave-safe bowl; cook,
uncovered, on HIGH (100%)
about 15 minutes or until
mixture is pulpy.
2 Add juice and sugar, stir
until sugar dissolves. Cook,
uncovered, on HIGH (100%)
about 20 minutes or until jam
jells when tested, stirring
3 times during cooking.
Pour into hot sterilised jars;
seal while hot.

spicy onion & tomato relish

6 medium (1.1kg) tomatoes, chopped
2 medium (300g) onions, chopped finely
2 medium (300g) apples, peeled, chopped finely
1 teaspoon salt
1 teaspoon finely grated lemon rind
1 teaspoon mustard powder
1 teaspoon garam masala
2 tablespoons mild curry powder
1¼ cups (250g) firmly packed brown sugar
½ cup (125ml) white vinegar
¼ cup (60ml) lemon juice
1 tablespoon tomato paste

1 Combine all ingredients in large glass microwave-safe bowl; cook, uncovered, on HIGH (100%) about 1 hour or until mixture thickens, stirring 3 times during cooking.
2 Spoon into hot sterilised jars; seal while hot.

- **prep time: 30 minutes**
- **cook time: 1 hour**
- **makes: about 1 litre**
- **storage: refrigerated for 2 months**
- **per serve: 0g fat; 15 cal**

sweet chilli tomato sauce

4 large (1kg) tomatoes, peeled, chopped
1 teaspoon salt
4 cloves garlic, chopped
¼ cup (60ml) balsamic vinegar
¼ cup (55g) sugar
¼ cup chopped fresh coriander leaves
3 small fresh red chillies, chopped

1 Combine all ingredients in large glass microwave-safe bowl. Cook, uncovered, on HIGH (100%) about 25 minutes or until sauce thickens, stirring twice during cooking; cool 5 minutes.
2 Blend or process sauce until smooth. Pour sauce into hot sterilised bottles; seal while hot.

- **prep time: 25 minutes**
- **cook time: 25 minutes**
- **makes: about 625ml**
- **storage: refrigerated for 2 weeks**
- **per serve: 0g fat; 6 cal**

green tomato relish

6 large (1.5kg) green
tomatoes, chopped

2 medium (300g) brown
onions, chopped

2 cloves garlic, crushed

1 cup (250ml) cider vinegar

¼ cup (60ml) malt vinegar

1 cup (220g) sugar

2 teaspoons salt

1 teaspoon ground ginger

4 cloves

½ teaspoon ground
cardamom

½ teaspoon ground
cinnamon

½ teaspoon ground turmeric

1 Combine all ingredients in large glass microwave-safe
bowl; cook, uncovered, on HIGH (100%) about 5 minutes or
until sugar dissolves, stirring 3 times during cooking.

2 Cook relish, uncovered, on HIGH (100%) about 1¼ hours
or until mixture thickens, stirring 3 times during cooking.

3 Spoon into hot sterilised jars; seal while hot.

- prep time: 20 minutes
- cook time: 1 hour
  20 minutes
- makes: about 1 litre
- storage: refrigerated for
  2 months
- per serve: 0g fat; 12 cal

dried fruit chutney

1 Combine dried fruits with the water in large glass microwave-safe bowl; cook, covered, on HIGH (100%) 10 minutes, stirring once during cooking. Stand, covered, 10 minutes. Add sugar, stir until sugar dissolves.
2 Add remaining ingredients; cook, uncovered, on HIGH (100%) about 30 minutes or until mixture is thick, stirring 3 times during cooking.
3 Spoon into hot sterilised jars; seal while hot.

200g chopped dried pears
200g chopped dried apricots
200g chopped pitted dates
180g chopped dried apples
240g sultanas
2 cups (500ml) water
2 cups (400g) firmly packed
  brown sugar
2 cups (500ml) cider vinegar
½ teaspoon chilli powder
½ teaspoon ground turmeric
½ teaspoon ground nutmeg
½ teaspoon ground ginger
1 clove garlic, crushed

- prep time: 25 minutes
- cook time: 50 minutes
- makes: about 1.75 litres
- storage: refrigerated for 2 months
- per serve: 0g fat; 25 cal

Glossary

bamboo shoots tender shoots of bamboo plants, available in cans; must be drained and rinsed before use.

bean sprouts also known as bean shoots; tender new growths of assorted beans and seeds germinated for consumption as sprouts.

beans

butter also known as lima beans, sold both dried and canned. A large beige bean having a mealy texture and mild taste.

kidney pink to maroon beans with a floury texture and fairly sweet flavour; sold dried or tinned.

bicarbonate of soda also called baking soda.

capers grey-green buds of a warm climate shrub sold either dried and salted or pickled in vinegar brine.

cardamom available in pod, seed or ground form. Has a distinctive, aromatic, sweetly rich flavour.

cayenne pepper thin-fleshed, long, very-hot red chilli; usually purchased dried and ground.

cheese

cream a soft cow's-milk cheese with a fat content ranging from 14 per cent to 33 per cent.

feta a crumbly textured goat's- or sheep's-milk cheese with a sharp, salty taste.

mozzarella a semi-soft cheese with a delicate, fresh taste; has a low melting point and stringy texture when hot.

parmesan a sharp-tasting, dry, hard cheese, made from skimmed or semi-skimmed milk and aged for at least a year.

chillies available in many types and sizes, both fresh and dried. The smaller the chilli, the hotter it is. Wear rubber gloves when handling chillies, as they can burn your skin. Removing seeds and membranes lessens the heat level.

chinese broccoli also known as gai lan.

chives related to the onion and leek, with subtle onion flavour.

chorizo a sausage of Spanish origin; made of coarsely ground pork and seasoned with garlic and chillies.

cinnamon dried inner bark of the shoots of the cinnamon tree; available as a stick or ground.

coconut

cream available in cartons and tins; as a rule, the proportions are two parts coconut to one part water.

desiccated unsweetened and concentrated, dried finely shredded coconut.

milk unsweetened coconut milk available in cans.

coriander fresh also known as cilantro or chinese parsley; bright-green-leafed herb with a pungent flavour.

cornflour also known as cornstarch; used as a thickening agent in cooking.

couscous a fine, grain-like cereal product, made from semolina.

cream we used fresh cream in this book, unless otherwise stated. It has no additives unlike commercially thickened cream. Minimum fat content 35%.

soured a thick commercially-cultured soured cream. Minimum fat content 35%.

cumin available both ground and as whole seeds; cumin has a warm, earthy, rather strong flavour.

curry powder a blend of ground spices; choose mild or hot to suit your taste and the recipe.

date fruit of the date palm tree, eaten fresh or dried, on their own or in prepared dishes.

fish sauce also called nam pla or nuoc nam; made from pulverised salted fermented fish, mostly anchovies. Has a pungent smell and strong taste; use sparingly.

five-spice powder a fragrant mixture of ground cinnamon, cloves, star anise, sichuan pepper and fennel seeds.

flat-leaf parsley also known as continental parsley or italian parsley.

garam masala a blend of spices based on varying proportions of cardamom, cinnamon, cloves, coriander, fennel and cumin, roasted and ground together. Black pepper and chilli can be added for a hotter version.

ginger also known as green or root ginger; the thick gnarled root of a tropical plant.

stem fresh ginger root preserved in sugar syrup.

gow gee wrappers also known as spring roll wrappers or wonton wrappers. Available from Asian food shops and some super-markets.

grand marnier a brandy-based orange-flavoured liqueur.

hoisin sauce a thick, sweet and spicy Chinese paste made from salted fermented soy beans, onions and garlic.

lentils many varieties of dried legumes, identified by and named after their colour.

mangetout (`eat all') also known as snow peas.

maple syrup distilled from the sap of maple trees found only in Canada and parts of North America.

milk, sweetened condensed a canned milk product consisting of milk with more than half the water content removed and sugar added to the milk that remains.

mixed spice a blend of ground spices usually consisting of cinnamon, allspice and nutmeg.

mushrooms

button small, cultivated white mushrooms with a delicate, subtle flavour.

chestnut brown mushrooms with mild, earthy flavour.

flat have a rich earthy flavour.

oyster also known as abalone; grey-white mushrooms shaped like a fan. Prized for their smooth texture and subtle, oyster-like flavour.

shiitake cultivated mushroom; has a rich, meaty flavour. Often sold dried.

mustard

dijon a pale brown, distinctively flavoured mild French mustard.

wholegrain a French-style coarse-grain mustard made from crushed mustard seeds and French dijon mustard.

oil

olive mono-unsaturated; made from the pressing of tree-ripened olives. Extra virgin and virgin are the best, obtained from the first pressings of the olive, while extra light or light refers to the taste, not fat levels.

sesame made from roasted, crushed, white sesame seeds; a flavouring rather than a cooking medium.

oregano also known as wild marjoram; has a woody stalk with clumps of tiny, dark green leaves that have a pungent, peppery flavour and are used fresh or dried.

oyster sauce rich sauce made from oysters and their brine, salt, soy sauce and starches.

pak choy also called pak choi or Chinese chard; has a mild mustard taste and is good braised or in stir-fries.

paprika ground dried red pepper (capsicum); available sweet, smoked or hot.

passionfruit also known as granadilla; a small tropical fruit with a tough dark-purple skin surrounding edible black sweet-sour seeds.

pecans golden-brown, buttery and rich nuts. Good in savoury and sweet dishes; especially good in salads.

pesto a paste made from fresh basil, oil, garlic, pine nuts and parmesan.

pine nuts also known as pignoli; small, cream-coloured kernels obtained from the cones of different varieties of pine trees.

plum sauce a thick, sweet and sour dipping sauce made from plums, vinegar, sugar, chillies and spices.

polenta a flour-like cereal made of ground corn.

pumpkin also known as squash; a member of the gourd family. Various types can be substituted for one another.

rice

arborio small, round-grain rice; especially suitable for risottos.

long grain elongated grain, remains separate when cooked; most popular steaming rice in Asia.

rolled oats traditional whole oat grains that have been steamed and flattened. Not the quick-cook variety.

sambal oelek a salty paste made from ground chillies.

soy sauce made from fermented soy beans; several variations are available.

sugar

brown an very soft, fine granulated sugar retaining molasses for its deep colour and flavour.

caster also known as superfine or finely granulated table sugar.

icing also known as confectioners' sugar or powdered sugar.

raw natural brown granulated sugar.

sweet chilli sauce mild, Thai sauce made from red chillies, sugar, garlic and vinegar.

tabasco sauce an extremely fiery sauce made from vinegar, hot red peppers and salt.

tahini paste made from crushed sesame seeds.

thyme a member of the mint family; has tiny grey-green leaves with a pungent minty, light-lemon aroma. Dried thyme comes in leaf and powdered forms.

turmeric a member of the ginger family, its root is dried and ground; pungent in taste but not hot.

vinegar

balsamic authentic only from the province of Modena, Italy; made from a regional white wine specially processed then aged in antique wooden casks to give the exquisite pungent flavour.

cider made from fermented apples.

malt made from fermented malt and beech shavings.

white made from spirit of cane sugar.

wine based on fermented red or white wine.

water chestnuts small brown tubers with a crisp, white, nutty-tasting flesh. Their crunchy texture is best experienced fresh, however, canned water chestnuts are more easily obtained.

worcestershire sauce a thin, dark-brown, spicy sauce used as seasoning for meat and gravies, and as a condiment.

Index

apple
 apple & pear crumble 91
 apple & pecan cake 97
 pork with caramelised apples 44
 tomato & apple jam 112
apricot
 apricot & passionfruit jam 109
 apricot citrus marmalade 107
artichokes 84
asian-style chilli drumsticks 31
asparagus 84
 fresh asparagus with hollandaise
  sauce 77
aubergine
 baba ghanoush 82
 caponata 83
 layered aubergine & tomato 73

baba ghanoush 82
bacon 11, 24
 bacon & cheese potatoes 67
 corn cobs with herb & bacon
  butter 69
 creamy broccoli & bacon
  pasta 60
 curried vegetable & bacon
  patties 51
 pasta carbonara 63
 potato & bacon casserole 68
beans 11, 12, 84
 chicken, bean & sausage
  casserole 32
 sweet chilli, sweet potato &
  bean toss 64
beef
 beef & nut biryani 37
 beef stock 22
 creamy beef stroganoff 38
 home-style meatloaf 39
 mulligatawny soup 20
beetroot 84
biryani, beef & nut 37
blueberry & lemon self-saucing
 pudding 92
broccoflower 84
broccoli 84
 broccoli with pine nuts 75
 creamy broccoli & bacon
  pasta 60
brussels sprouts 84
butternut squash see pumpkin

cabbage 84
cajun fish fillets with tabasco
 butter 48
cakes
 apple & pecan cake 97
 courgette walnut loaf 100
 moist carrot cake 98
 one-bowl chocolate cake 99
caponata 83

caramel sauce 94
carrots 84
 moist carrot cake 98
casseroles
 chicken, bean & sausage 32
 chilli chicken & chorizo 34
 potato & bacon 68
 ratatouille 53
cauliflower 84
 cauliflower au gratin 74
celeriac 84
cheese
 bacon & cheese potatoes 67
 cauliflower au gratin 74
 cheese & basil courgettes 72
 cheese & chive potatoes 66
 florentine chicken mozzarella 28
 macaroni cheese 62
 pasta carbonara 63
 salmon & pasta mornay 47
cheesecakes, strawberry-glazed
 89
chicken
 asian-style chilli drumsticks 31
 chicken & apricot tagine 27
 chicken & corn soup 16
 chicken & mushroom lasagne 61
 chicken minestrone 21
 chicken satay 35
 chicken stock 22
 chicken with lemon mustard
  sauce 24
 chicken with soy plum sauce 36
 chicken, bean & sausage
  casserole 32
 chilli chicken & chorizo
  casserole 34
 coq au vin 26
 florentine chicken mozzarella 28
 honey mustard chicken with
  fruity couscous 33
 tasty coated chicken 29
chickpeas
 chickpea & vegetable stuffed
  peppers 52
 curried chickpeas & rice 55
chilli chicken & chorizo casserole
 34
chilli garlic lamb with noodles 41
chocolate 86
 chocolate caramel slice 103
 mocha self-saucing pudding 93
 one-bowl chocolate cake 99
chowder, indian 17
christmas pudding 96
chutney, dried fruit 115
cinnamon cream 88
citrus butter 111
coconut lentil soup 15
combination short soup 12
cookies, peanut 102

coq au vin 26
corn 84
 chicken & corn soup 16
 corn cobs with herb & bacon
  butter 69
courgettes 84
 cheese & basil courgettes 72
 courgette walnut loaf 100
 crustless courgette quiche 59
couscous, fruity 33
cream cheese frosting 96
creamy beef stroganoff 38
creamy broccoli & bacon
 pasta 60
crumble, apple & pear 91
crustless courgette quiche 59
curries
 beef & nut biryani 37
 curried chickpeas & rice 55
 curried vegetable & bacon
  patties 51
 curried vegetable & rice
  medley 80
 lamb rogan josh 40
 mulligatawny soup 20
 quick lamb curry with mango
  relish 42
 spicy vegetable dhal 78
 thai-style chicken curry 30
 vegetable & split pea curry 56
custard 11, 86

dried fruit chutney 115

easy christmas pudding 96
easy fried rice 79
eggs
 poached 10
 scrambled 10

fennel 84
fish & seafood
 cajun fish fillets with tabasco
  butter 48
 risotto marinara 46
 salmon & pasta mornay 47
 singapore noodles 50
 tomato garlic prawns 49
florentine chicken mozzarella 28
fresh asparagus with hollandaise
 sauce 77
frittata, potato 54
frostings
 cream cheese 98
 fudge 99
fruit salad jam 110
fruity couscous 33

gai lan (Chinese broccoli) 85
greek-style mangetout 70
green tomato relish 114

home-style meatloaf 39
honey mustard chicken with fruity
    couscous 33

indian chowder 17

jams
    apricot & passionfruit 109
    fruit salad 110
    peach & passionfruit 106
    rhubarb berry 108
    tangy strawberry 112
    tomato & apple 112

kohlrabi 85

lamb
    chilli garlic lamb with noodles 41
    lamb rogan josh 40
    mustard lamb racks with
        sun-dried tomato crust 43
    quick lamb curry with mango
        relish 42
lasagne, chicken & mushroom 61
layered aubergine & tomato 73
lemon
    citrus butter 111
    lemon & blueberry self-saucing
        pudding 92
    lemon delicious 90
    lemon mustard sauce 24
lentils 11, 12
    coconut lentil soup 15
    spicy vegetable dhal 78

macaroni cheese 62
mangetout 85
    greek-style mangetout 70
mango relish 42
marmalade, apricot citrus 107
meatloaf, home-style 39
minestrone, chicken 21
mocha self-saucing pudding 93
moist carrot cake 98
muffins, pumpkin pecan 101
mulligatawny soup 20
mustard lamb racks with sun-dried
    tomato crust 43

nachos, vegetarian 58
noodles
    chilli garlic lamb with noodles 41
    satay pork noodles 45
    singapore noodles 50

one-bowl chocolate cake 99
onion & tomato relish 113

pak choy 85
    pak choy with mushrooms 76
parsnips 85
passionfruit
    apricot & passionfruit jam 109
    peach & passionfruit jam 106
pasta
    chicken & mushroom lasagne 61
    chicken minestrone 21

creamy broccoli & bacon
    pasta 60
macaroni cheese 62
pasta carbonara 63
pumpkin soup with tortellini 18
salmon & pasta mornay 47
patties, curried vegetable &
    bacon 51
pattypan squash 85
peach
    peach & passionfruit jam 106
    poached peaches & custard 86
peanut cookies 102
pear
    apple & pear crumble 91
    poached pears with cinnamon
        cream 88
peas 85
peppers
    chickpea & vegetable stuffed
        peppers 52
    warm pepper salad 71
poached peaches & custard 86
poached pears with cinnamon
    cream 88
pork
    combination short soup 12
    pork with caramelised apples 44
    satay pork noodles 45
    singapore noodles 50
    wontons 12
potatoes 85
    bacon & cheese potatoes 67
    cheese & chive potatoes 66
    jacket potatoes 11
    potato & bacon casserole 68
    potato frittata 54
prawns
    risotto marinara 46
    singapore noodles 50
    tomato garlic prawns 49
puddings
    easy christmas pudding 96
    lemon & blueberry self-saucing
        pudding 92
    mocha self-saucing pudding 93
    sticky toffee pudding 94
pumpkin 64, 85
    pumpkin pecan muffins 101
    pumpkin soup with tortellini 18

quiche, crustless courgette 59
quick lamb curry with mango
    relish 42

ratatouille casserole 53
relish
    green tomato 114
    mango 42
    spicy onion & tomato 113
rhubarb berry jam 108
rice
    curried chickpeas & rice 55
    curried vegetable & rice
        medley 80
    easy fried rice 79
    risotto marinara 46

risotto primavera 57
spinach rice 81
risotto see rice
rogan josh, lamb 40

salad, warm pepper 71
salmon & pasta mornay 47
satay
    chicken satay 35
    satay pork noodles 45
sauces
    caramel 94
    custard 11, 86
    hollandaise 77
    lemon mustard 24
    soy plum 36
    sweet chilli tomato 113
    white 11
sausage, chicken & bean
    casserole 32
seafood see fish & seafood
singapore noodles 50
slice, chocolate caramel 103
spicy onion & tomato relish 113
spicy vegetable dhal 78
spinach 85
    florentine chicken mozzarella 28
    spinach rice 81
sticky toffee pudding 94
stocks 22
strawberry
    strawberry-glazed cheesecakes
        89
    tangy strawberry jam 112
stroganoff, creamy beef 38
swedes 85
sweet chilli tomato sauce 113
sweet chilli, sweet potato & bean
    toss 64
sweet potato
    sweet chilli, sweet potato &
        bean toss 64
    sweet potato soup 14
swiss chard 85

tagine, chicken & apricot 27
tangy strawberry jam 112
tasty coated chicken 29
tat soi 85
thai-style chicken curry 30
tomato 10
    green tomato 114
    layered aubergine & tomato 73
    mustard lamb racks with
        sun-dried tomato crust 43
    spicy onion & tomato 113
    sweet chilli tomato sauce 113
    tomato & apple jam 112
    tomato garlic prawns 49
turnips 85

vegetable & split pea curry 56
vegetable soup with pesto 18
vegetarian nachos 58

warm pepper salad 71
white sauce 11

Conversion chart

measures

The cup and spoon measurements used in this book are metric: one measuring cup holds approximately 250ml; one metric tablespoon holds 20ml; one metric teaspoon holds 5ml.

All cup and spoon measurements are level. The most accurate way of measuring dry ingredients is to weigh them. When measuring liquids, use a clear glass or plastic jug with the metric markings.

We use large eggs with an average weight of 60g. This book contains recipes for dishes made with raw or lightly cooked eggs. These should be avoided by vulnerable people such as pregnant and nursing mothers, invalids, the elderly, babies and young children.

dry measures

METRIC	IMPERIAL
15g	½oz
30g	1oz
60g	2oz
90g	3oz
125g	4oz (¼lb)
155g	5oz
185g	6oz
220g	7oz
250g	8oz (½lb)
280g	9oz
315g	10oz
345g	11oz
375g	12oz (¾lb)
410g	13oz
440g	14oz
470g	15oz
500g	16oz (1lb)
750g	24oz (1½lb)
1kg	32oz (2lb)

liquid measures

METRIC	IMPERIAL
30ml	1 fluid oz
60ml	2 fluid oz
100ml	3 fluid oz
125ml	4 fluid oz
150ml	5 fluid oz (¼ pint/1 gill)
190ml	6 fluid oz
250ml	8 fluid oz
300ml	10 fluid oz (½ pint)
500ml	16 fluid oz
600ml	20 fluid oz (1 pint)
1000ml (1 litre)	1¾ pints

length measures

METRIC	IMPERIAL
3mm	⅛ in
6mm	¼in
1cm	½in
2cm	¾in
2.5cm	1in
5cm	2in
6cm	2½in
8cm	3in
10cm	4in
13cm	5in
15cm	6in
18cm	7in
20cm	8in
23cm	9in
25cm	10in
28cm	11in
30cm	12in (1ft)

oven temperatures

These oven temperatures are only a guide for conventional ovens. For fan-assisted ovens, check the manufacturer's manual.

	°C (CELSIUS)	°F (FAHRENHEIT)	GAS MARK
Very low	120	250	½
Low	150	275-300	1-2
Moderately low	160	325	3
Moderate	180	350-375	4-5
Moderately hot	200	400	6
Hot	220	425-450	7-8
Very hot	240	475	9

This book is published by Octopus Publishing Group Limited based on materials licensed it by ACP Magazines Ltd, a division of PBL Media Pty Limited

54 Park St, Sydney
GPO Box 4088, Sydney, NSW 2001
phone (02) 9282 8618;
fax (02) 9267 9438
acpbooks@acpmagazines.com.au;
www.acpbooks.com.au

OCTOPUS BOOKS

Design: Chris Bell
Food Director: Pamela Clark

Published and Distributed in the United Kingdom by Octopus Publishing Group Limited

Endeavour House
189 Shaftesbury Avenue
London WC2H 8JY
United Kingdom
phone + 44 (0) 207 632 5400;
fax + 44 (0) 207 632 5405

aww@octopusbooks.co.uk;
www.octopusbooks.co.uk
www.australian-womens-weekly.com

Printed and bound in China

International foreign language rights,
Brian Cearnes, ACP Books
bcearnes@acpmagazines.com.au

A catalogue record for this book is available from the British Library.

ISBN 978-1-907428-04-3
© ACP Magazines Ltd 2010
ABN 18 053 273 546

To order books:
telephone LBS on 01903 828 503
order online at www.australian-womens-weekly.com
or www.octopusbooks.co.uk

acp books